THE CONSERVATIVE GOVERNMENTS 1951–1964

The Conservative Governments 1951–1964

ANDREW BOXER

LONGMAN
LONDON AND NEW YORK

Addison Wesley Longman Limited
Edinburgh Gate
Harlow, Essex CM20 2JE, England
and Associated Companies throughout the world.

*Published in the United States of America
by Addison Wesley Longman Publishing Inc., New York*

©Addison Wesley Longman Limited 1996

First published 1996

ISBN 0582 209137 PPR

British Library Cataloguing in Publication Data

A catalogue record for this book is
available from the British Library

Library of Congress Cataloging-in-Publication Data

Boxer, Andrew
The conservative governments, 1951–1964 / Andrew Boxer
    p.   cm. -- (Seminar studies in history)
Includes bibliographical references and index.
ISBN 0-582-20913-7
1. Great Britain--Politics and government--1954–1964.
2. Conservatism--Great Britain--History--20th century.
3. Conservative Party (Great Britain) I. Title. II. Series
DA589.7.B69   1996
941.085--dc20   96-9287
                                                          CIP

Set by 7 in 10/12 Sabon
Produced through Longman Malaysia, CLP

CONTENTS

EDITORIAL FOREWORD

Such is the pace of historical enquiry in the modern world that there is an ever-widening gap between the specialist article or monograph, incorporating the results of current research, and general surveys, which inevitably become out of date. *Seminar Studies in History* are designed to bridge this gap. The books are written by experts in their field who are not only familiar with the latest research but have often contributed to it. They are frequently revised, in order to take account of new information and interpretations. They provide a selection of documents to illustrate major themes and provoke discussion, and also a guide to further reading. Their aim is to clarify complex issues without over-simplifying them, and to stimulate readers into deepening their knowledge and understanding of major themes and topics.

ROGER LOCKYER

NOTE ON REFERENCING SYSTEM

Readers should note that numbers in square brackets [5] refer them to the corresponding entry in the Bibliography at the end of the book (specific page numbers are given in italics). A number in square brackets preceded by Doc. [*Doc. 5*] refers readers to the corresponding item in the Documents section which follows the main text.

ACKNOWLEDGEMENTS

I would like to thank the Master and Fellows of Selwyn College, Cambridge for their generosity in granting me a bye-fellowship in 1992 and the President and Fellows of Trinity College, Oxford for making research facilities available.

This book is dedicated to Sue, Frances and Eleanor.

The publishers would like to thank the following for permission to reproduce copyright material: Blackwell Publishers for an extract from *Britain and the Suez Crisis* by D. Carlton published in 1988; The Labour Party for an extract from Hugh Gaitskill's speech, 1959; Weidenfeld and Nicolson for an extract from *Suez* by K. Kyle; Crown copyright is reproduced with the permission of the Controller of Her Majesty's Stationery Office; The Conservative Party Archives for an extract from Patrick Gordon Walker speaking on the radio and for an extract from a selection of letters sent to the Conservative Central Office showing public reaction to the Suez Crisis; Macmillan General Books for an extract from At the End of the Day 1961–1963, Memoirs, Volume 6, by Harold Macmillan.

Whilst every effort has been made to trace the owners of copyright material, in a few cases this has proved to be problematic and so we take this opportunity to offer our apologies to any copyright holders whose rights we may have unwittingly infringed.

PART ONE: CONSERVATIVE BRITAIN

1 DOMESTIC POLITICS

THE TORIES AND THEIR PREMIERS

The Conservatives came to power in October 1951 after one of Britain's more bizarre elections. The Labour Party received more votes than any other party in any general election until 1992, but won fewer seats than the Tories. Churchill returned to Downing Street, leading a government with an overall Commons majority of 17 [1]. The Conservative Party was in much better shape than it had been when it lost office in 1945. The huge Labour majority had been whittled down to just five seats in the election of 1950, and the Tories had used their years in opposition to revitalise their party organisation and membership and give a new gloss to their ideology [Doc. 1]. Their most important policy statement was *The Industrial Charter*, published in 1947. Advocating 'a system of free enterprise which is on terms with authority', it neatly reconciled traditional Tory values with the prevailing collectivist mood. It became the basis of a major restatement of Conservative thinking in *The Right Road for Britain*, published in 1949. By making clear that they accepted the welfare legislation and most of the nationalisation policy of the Labour governments, the Conservatives did not radically change their ideology but they did succeed in shedding the negative associations with the 1930s that had cost them dear in 1945. Nevertheless, their victory in 1951 owed less to their new image than to divisions within the Attlee government and middle-class disenchantment with the austerity of Labour rule.

Churchill's appointments reflected wartime nostalgia: he took on the Ministry of Defence himself, although he handed it on to a wartime colleague after a few months. Anthony Eden returned to the Foreign Office, and there were posts for some of the men from outside politics who had run departments during the war. Churchill tried to recreate something of the atmosphere of the War Cabinet by appointing three 'overlords' to coordinate the work of several departments and reduce the need for Cabinet and ministerial committees – an experiment that lasted only until 1953. The government was broadly based. The Liberal leader was offered, but declined, a post and, of those who had reshaped the party's strategy in opposition, R.A. Butler became Chancellor of the Exchequer and Harold Macmillan Minister of Housing. Both had served Churchill during the war and were advocates of a progressive Toryism that seemed to suggest a break with the past.

Churchill himself, at 77, was the oldest premier since Gladstone, but retained enormous prestige and authority. He admitted to finding the detail of government business irksome. 'In the last twenty-five years of peace and war, things have gotten (*sic*) ten or fifteen times more complicated. The problems I now have to face are much greater in numbers and complexity than they used to be' [79 *p. 34*]. Although undoubtedly past his prime, he retained his mastery of the Commons and led his government effectively, at least until his stroke in 1953. Preoccupied with foreign policy, he took less interest in domestic issues, although he was anxious to avoid industrial disputes and confrontation. He teased and exasperated Anthony Eden, his heir apparent, by constantly promising and then postponing retirement. Eden would probably have taken over in 1953 after Churchill's stroke had he not been recovering from a serious operation in the United States.

Eden finally succeeded Churchill in April 1955. He made few Cabinet changes, though these included the appointment of Macmillan to the Foreign Office. The two men did not get on well and Eden, like Churchill before him, wanted to be a Prime Minister who ran foreign policy himself. It was therefore no surprise when, in December 1955, Macmillan was moved to the Treasury, to be replaced as Foreign Secretary by the more compliant Selwyn Lloyd. After some hesitation, Eden decided on an election to consolidate his authority. The budget, produced two weeks after he took over, contained tax cuts to win over the voters. Eden need not have worried; his personal standing was high. The gramophone record of his election address produced by Tory Central Office may have sold only 20 copies, but the Conservatives increased their majority in the House of Commons to 54. The Tories won the election because increased consumer prosperity and the ending of rationing seemed to suggest that Conservative 'freedom' did indeed work better than socialist 'controls' and because the Labour Party, led by the ageing Clement Attlee, appeared divided.

Inevitably, assessments of Eden's record as Prime Minister focus largely on the Suez Crisis, but his government also faced some important industrial disputes and the growing problem of Commonwealth immigration, as well as colonial and European issues [35; 110]. Eden wished to continue the emollient 'one-nation' Toryism that had characterised Churchill's domestic policies. Ministers found his chairmanship of the Cabinet crisp and business-like and a welcome change from Churchill's discursive ramblings, but many have recorded their irritation at his constant telephone calls over niggling details. Although his three periods at the Foreign Office had given him enormous prestige as an international statesman, Eden knew little about domestic issues. He was sensitive to criticism and highly-strung, and the doubts about his capacity for leadership, which had been expressed in the past, surfaced again fairly early in his premiership. He was particularly stung by a *Daily Telegraph* article in January 1956 demanding the 'smack of firm government' [*Doc. 2*]. The need to appear tough undoubtedly influenced his handling of the Suez Crisis. Nor was he helped by the recurring fevers he suffered following his botched gall-bladder operation in April 1953.

When Eden resigned in January 1957 he was replaced by Harold Macmillan – principally because the Conservative Party did not want to appear to apologise for Suez by appointing R.A. Butler, who was known to have had reservations about it. Macmillan brought a more relaxed style to the business of government. He regularly stressed that he wanted it to be 'fun' and pinned to his secretaries' door a quotation from Gilbert and Sullivan's *The Gondoliers*: 'Quiet calm deliberation disentangles every knot' [33 *p. 13*]. Witty and urbane, he delighted in literary and historical analogies, sometimes to the exasperation of his ministers. One recalled that, in Cabinet, Macmillan could reach a decision even on such a mundane issue as rates 'via the Greek wars and Parnell' [63 *p. 118*]. Macmillan believed in letting ministers get on with their jobs, although he did interfere on issues about which he felt strongly. He was a consummate actor, who masked the disappointments of his private life and covered his inner uncertainties by cultivating an elegant, detached, sardonic but authoritative air and juxtaposing studied theatricality with a slightly old-fashioned aristocratic elegance. Macmillan's thinking about domestic politics had been shaped by his experiences as an MP in Stockton in the 1930s, and throughout his premiership he was more concerned about unemployment than inflation. Like his predecessors, he possessed an exaggerated view of Britain's influence in the world, but was more hard-headed than they in appraising that role. He believed that Britain's alliance with America was of paramount importance, and came to regard decolonisation and Britain's application to join the European Economic Commuity (EEC) as essential.

His premiership falls into two periods, neatly divided by the election of October 1959. In the first period Macmillan seemed in complete command. The Tory Party quickly recovered from the trauma of Suez, helped by the speed with which Macmillan restored Anglo-American relations. The Middle Eastern crisis of 1958 seemed almost to be a retrospective justification for Suez, and Macmillan was even able to turn the resignation of his Treasury ministers in January 1958 into a minor triumph by his phlegmatic (but carefully planned) description of it as 'a little local difficulty' [33 *p. 74*]. The seemingly inexorable growth of consumer affluence delivered the Conservatives an unprecedented third successive election victory, in which the government majority was once again increased, this time to 100. But things fell away rapidly as the new decade opened. The economy went from buoyancy to stagnation, and the government's increasingly interventionist methods of dealing with it were not only unsuccessful but sorted ill with the philosophy of the party of free enterprise. The relationship with America became very obviously one of dependence, not partnership, and the withdrawal from empire developed into such a hasty retreat that party unity was threatened. By-election losses, especially the spectacular loss of a safe Conservative seat in Orpington to the Liberals in March 1962, prompted Macmillan's ruthless Cabinet purge of July – known as the Night of the Long Knives – in which he dismissed no fewer than seven members of his Cabinet. Unfortunately, it reduced rather than enhanced his authority [51]. Liberal MP Jeremy Thorpe caught the public mood with his caustic comment: 'Greater love hath no man than this; that he lay down his friends for his life' [46 *p. 202*]. De Gaulle's rejection of Britain's application to join the EEC in January 1963 was a major blow, and Macmillan recorded in his diary: 'all our policies at home and abroad are in ruins' [33 *p. 447*].

His final year in power was overshadowed by revelations about security lapses and sex scandals. In September 1962, John Vassall, a clerk in the British embassy in Moscow, was exposed as a spy. His homosexuality had made him a victim of Soviet blackmail since 1956. Rumours circulated that Vassall had had an affair with Thomas Galbraith, a junior minister in Macmillan's government. Although innocent, Galbraith resigned and Macmillan regretted not having stood by him. Lurid press coverage of the case led to the establishment of a tribunal under Lord Radcliffe which exonerated Galbraith and other ministers of any involvement with Vassall. Two journalists, who refused to reveal to the tribunal the sources on which they had based their stories about Vassall, were imprisoned for six months. The press was able to wreak its revenge on Macmillan when a far more serious scandal broke in 1963.

With its salacious mixture of high-society corruption, sex and spying, the Profumo Affair appeared to suggest a society rotten at the top [*Doc. 3*]. John Profumo, the army minister, had had an affair in 1961 with a prostitute called Christine Keeler who was simultaneously seeing a Russian spy. Profumo denied the affair in the Commons in March 1963 and was publicly supported by Macmillan, still smarting from Galbraith's resignation. When in June Profumo confessed the truth, a prurient press and public revelled in the details. A Commons debate saw the government majority dwindle to 69, and one of the former Treasury ministers who had resigned in 1958 called for the Prime Minister to go. When Macmillan resigned in October 1963, albeit due to genuine ill health, his mordant comment was that he had never thought he could be 'brought down by two tarts' (a reference to Keeler and her call-girl colleague) [10 *p. 143*]. The Profumo Affair had sapped his confidence and eroded middle-class support for the government. In the increasingly libertarian, anti-establishment culture of the early 1960s, Macmillan and his government appeared anachronistic and out of touch. They were mercilessly lampooned by a new generation of satirists on television and in print. The appointment of the new Prime Minister discredited the methods by which the party chose its leader: as the front runners paraded themselves at the Party Conference in Blackpool, Macmillan schemed from his hospital bed to keep Butler out and ensure the appointment of Lord Home [*Doc. 4*].

The 14th Earl of Home took advantage of a recent Act of Parliament to renounce his title and sit in the House of Commons as Sir Alec Douglas-Home. His premiership was dominated by the imminent election. The bitterness of recent politics was reflected in the refusal of two members of Macmillan's government – Iain Macleod and Enoch Powell – to serve under him. Labour's new leader, Harold Wilson, derided Home's aristocratic background and economic illiteracy but, in the words of Kenneth Morgan, Home's 'very honesty and simplicity helped clear the foetid atmosphere' [17 *p. 228*]. His government's most notable decision was the abolition of resale price maintenance, by which manufacturers fixed the retail prices of their products. Although the aim was to encourage competition and reduce prices, many small traders who were Tory voters were outraged by it. The election of October 1964 was a close-run contest [1]. The Labour Party polled fewer votes than it had done in 1959 but emerged with an overall majority of five seats. The Tories had lost more than 1.7 million voters, many of whom had defected to the Liberals. The Tories had won three successive election victories in the 1950s because they appeared to be the party best able to satisfy middle-class aspirations to consumer affluence. When, in the 1960s, the economy turned sour and Conservative values became out of date, sufficient numbers deserted them to give the Labour Party a narrow victory.

DOMESTIC POLICIES: CONSENSUS AND CONSOLIDATION

The domestic policies of the four Prime Ministers of this period differed very little. They all subscribed to the Tory philosophy set out in the late 1940s, which accepted the welfare state and mixed economy established by the Labour governments. A return to the *laissez-faire* economic policies of the 1930s, with their concomitant high unemployment, was unthinkable, particularly in a decade of growing consumer prosperity. Like the Labour Party, the Conservatives wanted to maintain full employment and the benefits of the welfare state. By retaining what Macmillan called 'strategic control of the economy in the hands of the government' [36 *p. 302*], Tory policy was to promote affluence, industrial peace and the creation of a 'property-owning democracy'. It was succinctly summed up by one of Macmillan's ministers in 1957: 'If we can make everybody anxious to belong to a broadly based and prosperous middle class, we shall also bring a great many of the more successful Trade Unionists to our side' [48 *p. 229*]. Not only was this the key to short-term electoral success, but it was seen by the Tories as the best way of undermining the appeal of socialism. In the Cold War atmosphere of the 1950s, this meant more than victory over the Labour Party in a general election: although grossly exaggerated as a threat, the fear of communist influence on trade-union radicalism was very real.

   This explains why the Conservatives were wary of alienating trade-union leaders, most of whom were 'salt-of-the-earth types with silver hair and watch chains' [77 *p. 254*] and as much a part of the political establishment as ministers themselves. Churchill was determined to preserve industrial peace, even if it meant giving in to potentially inflationary wage demands. He appointed Sir Walter Monckton as Minister of Labour and instructed him to avoid conflict with the unions. Monckton had entered Parliament only in February 1951 and did not really consider himself a Conservative Party politician; to preserve his image as a neutral conciliator he even refused invitations to speak at Tory conferences. Two rail strikes, in 1953 and 1954, were averted by capitulation to the men's terms and, although the government was prepared to use existing law to deal with unofficial strikes that threatened vital services, any new legislation that risked confrontation with the Trades Union Congress (TUC) was ruled out. When Eden contemplated legislation to curb industrial action after the rail and dock strikes of 1955, Monckton demurred, warning that 'any government initiative in the field of industrial relations should carry the greatest possible measure of TUC approval and concurrence. Unless we carry with us the responsible elements, who are at present in a majority, we run the risk of uniting the whole movement against us.' He concluded: 'there is no panacea for these ills and, in particular, the scope for remedial action by the government is limited' [110 *p. 26*]. Eden was persuaded [*Doc. 5*].

The generally harmonious relationship between government and unions began to change in the mid-1950s. So, too, did public attitudes. The 1955 rail strike was the first national stoppage for some years to cause serious inconvenience to the public and, in the second half of the decade, the number of working days lost increased from 2.4 million in 1954 to 8.4 million in 1957. In 1956 Frank Cousins became leader of the Transport and General Workers' Union (TGWU) and abandoned the moderate stance of his predecessors. He persuaded the 1957 TUC Conference to reject wage-restraint in any form, and his policy of encouraging pay deals to be negotiated on the shop floor, rather than being imposed by national union officials, gave power to militant shop stewards. Communist control of the Electricians' Union became a *cause célèbre* and contributed to the increasingly hostile public perception of trade unions. Macmillan's approach to industrial unrest was initially the same as that of his predecessors. Although he declared to the Cabinet in November 1957 that 'we shall refuse to create more money to finance wage awards which are not matched by increased output' [33 *p. 68*], the industrial troubles of 1957 and 1958 forced him into concessions to the railwaymen and negotiation with the TUC leaders to head off other disputes. In 1961 his government attempted a more resolute approach and tried to control inflation by an incomes policy. But this was gravely weakened by the ability of powerful unions – the electricians in 1961 and the dockers in 1962 – to achieve pay increases that breached government guidelines. Trade-union opposition also torpedoed Macmillan's efforts at economic planning in 1962. The TUC response to the National Economic Development Council (NEDC) was lukewarm and they joined it only reluctantly, fearful that it might prove an instrument of wage restraint, and flatly refused cooperation with the National Incomes Commission (NIC), despite its lack of statutory powers.

All four Tory governments fought shy of trade-union legislation. This has been criticised by even the most sympathetic commentators.

> The Ministry of Labour's reluctance to tackle the necessary task of reforming restrictive labour practices contributed substantially to the problems of industry. Survey after survey noted the under-utilization of capital, overmanning, the shortage of certain skills, the failure to reform apprenticeship, as well as the more publicized evils of demarcation disputes and wildcat strikes. [63 *p. 136*]

These problems were ignored not just because the government lacked the stomach for what would have been a bitter battle, but because their concept of 'one-nation Toryism' aimed at consensus rather than confrontation. A similar motive influenced housing policy. If Conservative governments could outbuild their Labour predecessors, the growth of the 'property-owning democracy' would, it was hoped, erode working-class support for the left. This is why Macmillan, who became Churchill's housing minister in 1951, was given the ambitious target of building 300,000 houses a year, a figure deliberately chosen to outbid Labour's promise of 200,000. This was not just a cynical piece of party politics. Much of the post-war fervour for building the 'New Jerusalem' remained. The widely held belief that better housing was one of the keys to reducing poverty, crime and ill health was part of what John Stevenson calls the 'faith in modern planning as the panacea for all the ills of industrial society' [12 *pp. 89–90*].

The 1952 Housing Act increased the subsidies paid to local authorities and gave more licences to private house-builders. In 1953 Macmillan was able to boast of 319,000 new houses and in 1954 of a record 348,000. This, given the economic difficulties of the early 1950s, was no mean feat. However, as John Turner points out, 'he achieved great things by concentrating on his own mission, ignoring any consequences this might have for anything else' [48 *p. 82*].

Macmillan benefited from Churchill's support in his battle with the Treasury for money, but his success in earmarking resources for housing may well have damaged industrial development. Subsequent Housing Acts reduced the subsidy to local authorities for general house-building to encourage them to concentrate on slum clearance and the provision of accommodation for needy groups. Thus, in keeping with Tory philosophy, government policy by the late 1950s was primarily directed towards private building and the improvement of existing stock. Between 1951 and 1964, approximately three million houses were built and by 1965 47 per cent of households lived in owner-occupied property.

This was an impressive record, but did not cure the shortage, because the increase in the population, combined with rapid social change, ensured that demand ran ahead of supply. In an effort to tackle the problem by encouraging more landlords to rent, the 1957 Rent Act removed more than 800,000 houses from rent control and allowed rent increases for over four million which remained controlled. The Act was attacked by the Labour Party as a charter for unscrupulous landlords, but the fuss died down when it became apparent that it had fulfilled neither the best hopes of the government nor the worst fears of the opposition. Local authorities, in pursuit of a speedy solution to a pressing problem, began building tower blocks which required less space in crowded cities and were cheaper than houses for an equivalent number of tenants. Tower-block developments reached their peak in the mid-1960s, by which time there was already widespread disillusionment with them. Doubts about housing policy, slum clearance and the soulless products of urban planning contributed to the mood of disenchantment with the Tory government that prevailed in the early 1960s. One of the by-products of the Profumo Affair was the exposure of Peter Rachman, who had made himself a fortune by purchasing property due for redevelopment and using brutal methods to expel sitting tenants. He seemed to typify an age in which more than 100 property speculators had made themselves millionaires by exploiting Conservative legislation to create a free market in development land.

In a number of areas the Conservative governments were content to maintain the policy of their Labour predecessors. In education there was expansion at secondary and tertiary level but no radical reform. Although more teachers were trained and the number of sixth-form pupils doubled, there was continued concern about class sizes, the quality of school buildings and the number of degree-trained teachers, especially in the inner cities. Between 1959 and 1963 there were six government reports on aspects of education. This reflected public interest in the issue and growing official concern about Britain's poor economic performance relative to her principal competitors. The 11-plus examination, which determined whether children went to a grammar school or a secondary modern, was increasingly regarded as socially divisive and inefficient, even among some Tory supporters. The Conservatives wanted to keep grammar schools and resisted the pressure coming from some local authorities and the Labour Party to introduce comprehensives, for which the 11-plus was unnecessary. Two reports – in 1959 and 1963 – recommended raising the school-leaving age to 16, and the government announced that this would occur in 1970–71. Responding to the growing demand for higher education, the government founded seven new universities and increased the number of students in full-time higher education from 122,000 in 1955 to 216,000 in 1963 [3]. Following a White Paper in 1956 which recommended the expansion of technical education, colleges of advanced technology were created, and in October 1963 the government accepted the Robbins Report on higher education which recommended a doubling of university places in ten years and the development of the colleges of advanced technology into technological universities.

In opposition, the Conservatives had criticised supposedly wasteful expenditure on the administration of the welfare system, but in government they treated it with reverence. The Guillebaud Committee was established in 1953 to report on the cost of the NHS, but found that 'any charge that there has been widespread extravagance in the National Health Service (NHS), whether in respect of the spending of money or the use of manpower, is not borne out by our evidence' [2 *p. 167*]. Pensions and national assistance benefits continued to rise, as did prescription charges, but hospital building was neglected until 1962, when a major rebuilding programme was announced. It was an indication of the uncontroversial nature of the NHS during this period that the Minister of Health did not sit in the Cabinet between 1952 and 1962.

Modernising Britain's transport system was only belatedly addressed. The first motorways were opened in the early 1960s, and in February 1963 the Beeching Report recommended the closure of 5,000 miles of railway and more than 2,300 stations. Beeching's measures aroused fierce controversy because, instead of being part of a coordinated transport policy, they were designed merely to reduce costs and ignored the social consequences of eliminating rural railway lines [66].

The Conservatives kept under public ownership all the industries and utilities nationalised by the Attlee governments, with the exception of road haulage and iron and steel, but even in these a measure of state control was retained. The BBC monopoly of television broadcasting was ended in 1954, but a determined campaign was waged against commercial television by those fearful of the effect it would have on broadcasting standards and public morals. 'For the sake of our children, we should resist it,' opined the Archbishop of York [10 *p. 74*]. Their worst fears were not realised, and competition from ITV stimulated innovation in its rival. It was the BBC that pioneered satire on television with *That Was the Week That Was*, a programme launched in November 1962 which mercilessly ridiculed the government and contributed to the iconoclastic culture developing in the early 1960s.

British society became marginally more liberal in the 1950s, and some government initiatives reflected this. Disquiet over capital punishment grew as a result of some miscarriages of justice, and a Private Member's Bill to abolish it was even passed by the Commons in 1956 but rejected by the Lords. The 1957 Homicide Act abolished the death penalty for certain degrees of murder but, although Home Secretary Butler soon found the Act to be almost unworkable, total abolition did not occur until 1965. The Wolfenden Report of 1957 recommended legalising homosexual acts between consenting adults, but Butler was not prepared to confront the hostility of Tory MPs by legislating on the issue [34]. This, too, had to await a Labour majority in the Commons. Butler did act on Wolfenden's other recommendation, and the Street Offences Act of 1959 made it illegal for prostitutes to solicit on the streets. The Obscene Publications Act of the same year was an attempt to protect serious authors and publishers from obscenity charges. Butler was also responsible for some important measures of penal reform, although the liberal reputation he thus acquired alienated right-wing Tory opinion and undermined his chances of succeeding Macmillan.

Less tolerant was the British response to the growing problem of Commonwealth immigration. In a bid to make the Commonwealth a meaningful entity, the Labour government in 1948 had passed the British Nationality Act which, in effect, gave British citizenship to nearly 1,000 million people in the Commonwealth and Empire. The

United States tightened its immigration laws in 1952, which made Britain, with its full employment and welfare-state benefits, an attractive destination for West Indians anxious to escape domestic poverty, especially as ever-cheaper travel made the journey possible. Statistically, the problem was insignificant. Only 12,000 more people came into Britain than left it between 1951 and 1961 and, in the period 1951–84, Britain was a net exporter of population to the tune of nearly half a million [3]. By 1961 there were approximately 300,000 immigrants from the West Indies and the Indian sub-continent living in Britain, a figure dwarfed by the number of Irish from the Republic, who were the largest single immigrant group in the 25 years after the war.

Both the Churchill and the Eden governments were worried about the problem of coloured immigration, but fought shy of legislation [*Doc. 6*]. There was a number of complications. No one wanted to restrict immigration from the Republic of Ireland or the white communities in the former dominions, but it was feared that discriminatory legislation against blacks and Asians would be controversial in Britain and offensive to Commonwealth opinion. The numbers coming in were relatively small and jobs were plentiful. Nevertheless, there had been some racial violence in London in October 1954, and three months later ministers had to head off a Private Member's Bill to restrict immigration. Lord Swinton, the Commonwealth Secretary, summed up the government's attitude in 1954 in a letter to Lord Salisbury. 'If we legislate on immigration, though we can draft it in non-discriminatory terms, we cannot conceal the obvious fact that the object is to keep out coloured people. Unless there is a really strong case for this, it would surely be an unwise moment to raise the issue when we are preaching, and trying to practise, partnership, and the abolition of the colour bar' [7 *p. 299*]. There were more serious race riots in August 1958 in London's Notting Hill and in Nottingham, prompting demands for action at the Tory Conference in October. In the 1959 election Oswald Mosley tried to use the immigration issue to resurrect his political career. He stood for Parliament demanding compulsory free repatriation of West Indians, and appealed to vulgar prejudice by suggesting that black workers would accept lower wages because they could live on a daily diet of a tin of cat food. He lost his deposit.

The increase in immigration in 1960 and early 1961 spurred the government into action. Butler concluded in May 1961 that 'it was now accepted by government supporters that some form of control was unavoidable if we were not to have a colour problem in this country on a similar scale to the USA' [66 *p. 420*]. In April 1962 the Commonwealth Immigrants Act was passed. Skilled workers, and those with a job to go to, continued to have free access. The remainder were subject to government-controlled quotas. The Labour and Liberal Parties condemned the Act as racialist because white immigrants would not be affected; nor, since it only applied to the Commonwealth, would unskilled Irish labourers. The Labour Party's opposition to the Act landed them in trouble with some of their own supporters, since it was working-class people in the cities where immigrants congregated who felt most threatened by them [*Doc. 7*]. One of the few gains made by the Conservatives in the 1964 election was in Smethwick, where Patrick Gordon-Walker was defeated by a Tory candidate whose supporters had used a racialist campaign slogan: 'if you want a nigger neighbour, vote Labour' [12 *p. 219*]. Once in office, Labour, far from repealing the 1962 Act, tightened controls still further.

THE LABOUR PARTY: A HOUSE DIVIDED

In the 1950s the Labour Party was divided over policy and ideology. There were bitter rows in Parliament and at Party Conferences. The party lost three elections in a row, and some commentators wondered whether they could ever win another. Individual membership fell by 20 per cent and 1,700,000 voters deserted between 1951 and 1964 [1].

The contemporary explanation for this decline was the growing consumer affluence of the 1950s that was thought to have broken up the cohesion and class solidarity of Britain's traditional working class. The sudden availability of consumer goods after the austerity and rationing of Labour's years in power had, it seemed, turned a solid phalanx of potential Labour Party voters into owners of middle-class comforts who regarded the Conservative Party as the providers and guardians of their new-found status and aspirations. Richard Crossman, reflecting on defeat in the 1955 general election, felt that Labour was 'ideologically disintegrated by the fact that Keynesian welfare capitalism is providing, for the time being, quite an adequate substitute for socialism' [41 *p. 437*]. Bessie Braddock, the Labour MP for Liverpool Exchange, was more earthy: 'Right now the basic insecurity the workers feel is this: they are haunted by the spectre of the van driving to the door to take away the TV set' [14 *p. 44*].

However, it would be rash to assume too close a causal connection between growing consumer affluence and Labour unpopularity. The party's electoral performance in the 1930s was even worse than in the 1950s, and the sociological changes that had taken place in Britain in the 1950s did not prevent them from winning the general elections of 1964 and 1966. Clearly, social trends had some impact on voting behaviour, but it is difficult to determine how much, and impossible to identify precisely how far they were responsible for Labour's decline in electoral appeal. Other factors were also important.

By 1950 much of what the Labour government had set out to achieve in 1945 had been accomplished, and they seemed to have run out of appealing ideas. They held on to power in the 1950 election, but with their majority reduced from 146 seats to just five. During the 1950–51 administration the problems and disputes that were to bedevil the Labour Party in the 1950s began to emerge. Aneurin Bevan, the Minister of Health who had created the National Health Service, was twice passed over for promotion. He particularly resented the Chancellorship going to the relatively young and inexperienced Hugh Gaitskell, and in April 1951 he resigned in protest against the budget.

The clash between Gaitskell and Bevan in 1951 sparked a personal feud that smouldered on until they patched up an uneasy alliance in 1956, but it was also a struggle for the leadership and soul of the party. In 1951 Attlee was 68 and his retirement was imminent. Gaitskell and Bevan were the leaders of the next generation, but their backgrounds, personal style and convictions were from opposite traditions. Bevan, from the Welsh town of Tredegar, had been a coal-miner and trade-union official. For him, the achievements of 1945 to 1951 had been a start, a beginning on the road to a socialist society, and he was impatient with the cautious leadership of the Labour Party. In a speech in February 1956 he said: 'When you join a team in the expectation that you are going to play rugger, you can't be expected to be enthusiastic if you are asked to play tiddlywinks' [28 *p. 500*]. And yet, for all his fiery oratory and radical zeal, Bevan found it hard to formulate a coherent set of policies, and 'Bevanism' was more a matter of personal loyalty to his charismatic personality than a political creed. Bevan's protest coincided with, and was to some extent sustained by, an upsurge in individual membership of the Labour Party in the early 1950s. Many of these new members, who looked to Bevan and his parliamentary caucus for leadership, wanted the party to commit itself to radical socialism. The decline in party membership which began in 1953 helps to explain the break-up of the Bevanite parliamentary group [64]. Gaitskell, on the other hand, was part of a middle-class, public-school and university-educated group of Labour leaders who had come to the workers' party out of conscience and intellectual conviction. To them, the job of the Labour Party in opposition was to act responsibly, win back the middle-class voters who had deserted them in 1950 and 1951, and rescue the welfare state and mixed economy created by the Attlee administrations from mismanagement by the Conservatives.

In March 1952 Bevan led 57 MPs in a revolt against the party's line on rearmament. This began the so-called Bevanite 'movement', and in the 1952 Party Conference his supporters won six out of the seven constituency party seats on the National Executive Committee (NEC), reflecting the strength of support for the left among rank-and-file members. A more serious row occurred in April 1954, when Bevan resigned from the Shadow Cabinet in protest against the decision of the Parliamentary Labour Party (PLP) to support the government's policy on German rearmament and the establishment of the South-East Asia Treaty Organisation (SEATO). At the Party Conference of that year he lashed out at what he saw as the failings of the leadership: 'The right kind of leader for the Labour Party is a desiccated calculating machine who must not in any way permit himself to be swayed by indignation. If he sees suffering, privation or injustice he must not allow it to move him, for that would be evidence of the lack of proper education or of absence of self-control' [23 *p. 293*]. It is not clear whether Bevan was referring to Attlee or Gaitskell; the latter had just defeated Bevan in an election for the post of Party Treasurer and was clearly being groomed by the right-wing forces in the party to succeed Attlee as leader. The conference, however, only narrowly voted to endorse the PLP line on German rearmament. Bevanite protest was wounding the party. Churchill is said to have purred to his doctor, 'That fellow is a gold mine to us', when he heard the news of Bevan's speech [40 *p. 633*].

In March 1955 Bevan and a group of 62 Labour MPs abstained from a motion in the House of Commons on the manufacture of a British hydrogen bomb. Bevan interrupted Clement Attlee's speech to seek clarification of British policy about the use of the bomb. Neither Churchill nor Attlee was willing to define the exact circumstances under which nuclear weapons would be used, since this would indicate to the USSR how far it could go without provoking a NATO nuclear strike. Bevan wanted it made clear whether 'we should use thermonuclear weapons in circumstances of hostilities, although they were not used against us' [4, 537 *col. 2176*]. For Attlee and the Labour Party leadership, Bevan's protest was highly irresponsible. It was also seen as gross defiance of the leadership – not only had the Bevanites defied party discipline, but Bevan had embarrassed and insulted his leader. The PLP voted 141 to 112 to withdraw the party whip from Bevan, but the NEC voted 14–13 not to expel him from the party.

These very public divisions contributed to the general election defeat of May 1955 in which the Labour Party lost 18 seats and recorded 1,500,000 fewer votes than in 1951 [1]. In an effort to identify the causes of their election defeat the Labour Party established a committee, chaired by Harold Wilson, to undertake a systematic investigation of its local organisation. The report was damning. 'Compared with our opponents', wrote Wilson, 'we are still at the penny-farthing stage in a jet-propelled era, and our machine, at that, is getting rusty . . . with age' [43 *p. 194*]. But few of Wilson's recommendations were implemented. In December 1955 Attlee retired after 20 years as leader of the party. It was the job of the PLP to vote for his successor. Herbert Morrison, who clearly expected to be elected, was thought by most MPs to be too old. The party rallied to the younger Hugh Gaitskell; to the right wing he was the obvious leader, although there were many who voted for him because they disliked and feared Bevan. In the event, Gaitskell won on the first ballot with 157 votes to 70 for Bevan and only 40 for Morrison.

Gaitskell's first major test as leader came with the Suez Crisis of 1956. His policy was much criticised at the time and since. He was accused of inconsistency because, although in the Commons debate on 2 August he compared Nasser with Mussolini and Hitler, he nevertheless rejected any attack on Egypt unless sanctioned by the United Nations. In his television broadcast on 4 November, the day before British troops went into action, he denounced Britain's use of force and called on the dissident Tories to remove Eden. The Conservative Party and sections of the press retaliated by calling him unpatriotic and even traitorous. In electoral terms Gaitskell gained nothing from Suez; Eden's personal popularity, as measured by Gallup, went up during the crisis. On the other hand, Suez consolidated Gaitskell's leadership of the Labour Party and helped to bridge the gulf between himself and Bevan. The intensity of Labour criticism of the government probably helped weaken Eden's resolve, hastening the collapse of his policy.

By the end of 1956 Bevan and Gaitskell were working well together and Bevan became the Shadow Foreign Secretary. His iconoclastic crusade now over, Bevan startled his supporters by an apparent about-face at the 1957 Party Conference. He argued for the retention of a British independent nuclear bomb, without which any future Foreign Secretary would be walking 'naked into the conference chamber . . . to preach sermons' [28 *p. 574*]. This was not a complete reversal of his previous position; rather, he was now arguing for multilateral disarmament and opposing a unilateralist motion. When he had visited the USSR in September, Khrushchev had made it clear to him that Britain's unilateral disarmament would be seen in the USSR as no more than an empty gesture. Khrushchev had even hinted that Britain had a role to play in restraining American and German belligerence towards the USSR. The Brighton Conference of 1957 signalled the end of Bevan's opposition to the party leadership, but it did not end the divisions within the party. Ironically, it was to be Gaitskell himself who, after the 1959 election, was to cause even deeper divisions.

In the 1959 general election Gaitskell and the Labour Party fought a good campaign. Opinion polls showed support for the government flagging. Even Macmillan acknowledged this: 'The Socialists had a very successful TV (*sic*) last night – much better than ours. Gaitskell is becoming very expert' [38 *p. 8*]. Gaitskell was, however, trapped into one costly campaign blunder when he promised that Labour's spending plans could be financed without an increase in income tax. Since a campaign leaflet also promised that the Labour Party would reduce purchase tax, the Tories were able to depict Gaitskell as shamelessly endeavouring to bribe the electorate by offering to spend more without raising taxes. The party suffered their third consecutive electoral defeat, losing another 19 seats.

Gaitskell now became convinced that the party needed to rethink their ideology if they were ever again to achieve power. In particular, he was convinced that Labour's commitment to nationalisation was unpopular and out of date. This was exactly the conclusion that Anthony Crosland had reached in his book *The Future of Socialism*, published in 1956: 'Is it not then clear that ownership of the means of production has ceased to be the key factor which imparts to a society its essential character?' [9 *p. 90*]. Gaitskell endorsed this verdict and believed that the Labour Party should be honest enough to do so too, by removing from its constitution Clause Four, which committed the party to further nationalisation. As a result, he plunged the party once more into civil war, made all the more bitter by his own personality and tactics. Once convinced of a course of action, he was not a man to shirk the dangers. 'Gaitskell led from the front, going over the top to confront the enemy like a regimental officer leading his men to mass slaughter at the battle of the Somme' [69 p. 221]. While this could be regarded as politically courageous, it also displayed a streak of stubbornness that alienated his opponents and made him temperamentally unsuited to the task of straightening out the labyrinthine complexities of Labour Party ideology. The struggle also revealed Gaitskell's misunderstanding of the psychology of many members of his party. For those born into the working class, who had fought their way up through the labour movement, the Labour Party was a lifelong commitment, to which they were attached with a quasi-religious zeal. 'We were being asked to take Genesis out of the Bible. You don't have to be a fundamentalist to say that Genesis is part of the Bible', explained Harold Wilson [43 p. 227].

When the party gathered in Blackpool in November 1959 for its annual conference, what Ben Pimlott calls Gaitskell's 'elephantine clumsiness' [43 p. 225] had contributed in large measure to an atmosphere in which the party leadership, according to Crossman, was 'stinking with intrigue and suspicion' [41 p. 802]. Gaitskell's conference speech went down badly and he was attacked for promoting disunity [Doc. 8]. His critics on the left wanted the party to commit itself with crusading zeal to socialism, not rewrite its constitution. To Gaitskell and his supporters it seemed as if the left-wingers were wedded to obsolete party dogmas and out of touch with the material aspirations of ordinary voters. Gaitskell was forced to back down over Clause Four, and in March 1960 he accepted a compromise worked out by the NEC by which Clause Four remained and a statement of 'clarification' was added. But the episode had done him considerable damage because, in seeking to alter the party's image, he had antagonised not only the left of the party, but also the conservative-minded trade-union leaders who had hitherto been his strongest supporters in his battles with the Bevanites.

In 1960 Britain's independent nuclear deterrent once again became an issue of national politics. In April the government made public the decision to cancel the Blue Streak missile, which meant that Britain would have to rely on an American missile to deliver the British bomb. This raised the question of how independent the British deterrent really was. Whether it was morally right for Britain, or any other nation for that matter, to possess nuclear weapons at all had been an issue of left-wing politics for some time and had been brought into public prominence by the formation in February 1958 of the Campaign for Nuclear Disarmament (CND). A series of well-publicised, popular marches from the nuclear weapons plant at Aldermaston to Trafalgar Square in London had begun in April 1958 and had attracted bigger crowds at each succeeding Easter. As many as 100,000 people are estimated to have attended the rally in Trafalgar Square on 18 April 1960 – just five days after the announcement cancelling Blue Streak. In May the acrimonious termination of the Paris summit between Khrushchev and Eisenhower increased international tension and alarm about the possible use of nuclear weapons.

Typically, Gaitskell regarded the issue as one of national, not just internal Labour Party politics. His biographer states: 'Labour's crisis in 1960 . . . was a conflict about its character: whether the Party was to be a protest movement or a prospective government of the country' [49 *p. 335*]. Gaitskell argued that unilateral disarmament by Britain would have no impact in persuading the USSR or the USA to reduce their nuclear arsenals. He also believed it would be dishonest for Britain to claim a morally righteous position by abandoning nuclear weapons while at the same time remaining within NATO and expecting the USA to use them in Britain's defence. His opponents argued that, in a dangerous world, a gesture by Britain could help to allieviate tension and begin the disarmament process. Some went further and argued that Britain should withdraw from the NATO alliance.

During 1960 a number of trade-union conferences voted in favour of unilateral disarmament, and it became clear that Gaitskell's views, and perhaps also his leadership, would be threatened at the Party Conference in the autumn. When the Labour Party met at Scarborough in October, Gaitskell probably won the support of most of the delegates in the hall, but trade-union block votes ensured that the conference voted by the small majority of 300,000 for a unilateralist defence policy.

The Labour Party was now in serious difficulties. Its leader had been defeated on a major issue of policy by the Party Conference. Furthermore, the party was now committed to a policy which commanded little support in the PLP. Macmillan was quick to make political capital out of this, 'As I understand it,' he remarked in the House of Commons, 'the defence policy of the Party opposite depends on the chance vote of a delegate conference of the National Union of Railwaymen' [4, 626 *col. 1601*]. On 20 October Harold Wilson announced that he intended to challenge Gaitskell for the leadership of the party, arguing that only a new leader could reunite it. But Wilson was regarded by many as no more than an opportunist [*Doc. 9*]. On 3 November Gaitskell was re-elected by 166 votes to 81, but a third of the PLP had indicated their unhappiness with his leadership.

Nevertheless, the party's recovery was fairly rapid. In 1961 three of the biggest unions – the shopworkers (USDAW), the engineers (AEU) and the railwaymen (NUR) – changed their decision about the bomb. Of the major unions this left only the transport workers (TGWU), led by Frank Cousins, continuing their commitment to unilateral disarmament. Peter Clarke explains how the reversal was achieved. 'The fact that the block vote could be brought into line on defence can be attributed to familiarity with the issue, loyalty to the leadership, anti-communism and, not least, a lot of business in smoke-filled rooms' [56 *p. 255*]. Gaitskell's cause was also assisted by the formation in November 1960 of the Campaign for Democratic Socialism. This had been founded by allies of Gaitskell who wanted to see the Scarborough decision reversed, and its members set about rallying support for the leadership in the trade unions and constituency parties. The result was a decisive defeat for unilateralism (by 4.5 million votes to 1.7 million) at the party's Conference in Blackpool in October 1961. Gaitskell scored a second victory when the conference rejected Cousins's attempt to commit the party to further nationalisation.

With the Conservatives in difficulties in 1962, the Labour Party once again began to look like an alternative administration. When Macmillan's government had made a formal application for membership of the European Economic Community (EEC) in August 1961, Gaitskell was lukewarm about entry but felt on balance that Britain would benefit from membership. He said on television in May 1962: 'To go in on good terms would, I believe, be the best solution. . . . Not to go in would be a pity, but it would not be a catastrophe' [49 *p. 400*]. However, he was also wary of splitting the party once again. He had told a Labour policy conference in December 1961: 'I do not want another internal party row about this' [49 *p. 393*]. This explains what Peter Clarke calls his 'uncharacteristically ambivalent, fence-sitting attitude' [56 *p. 255*] on the issue. By the time of the Party Conference at Brighton in October 1962, Gaitskell had come out firmly against Britain's entry, denouncing the terms that Macmillan had negotiated as 'the end of a thousand years of history' [49 *p. 404*].

In January 1963 Gaitskell unexpectedly died of a rare

immunological disease. George Brown, deputy leader of the party since 1960, following Bevan's death, expected to be elected leader. For some Labour MPs, however, Brown was too right-wing, and for others he was too volatile. 'Are we going to be led by a neurotic drunk?' wailed Anthony Crosland [43 *p. 255*]. Brown's principal rival was Harold Wilson, who had enough of a Bevanite past to appease the left of the party and whose successful criticisms of the government as Shadow Chancellor had given him national stature. Wilson won on the second ballot and George Brown, as acting leader, had the unhappy task of announcing his own defeat.

Harold Wilson proved to be an extremely successful Leader of the Opposition. He projected an image 'of self-help, energy, efficiency and hostility to upper-class pretension and privilege', writes his biographer, Ben Pimlott [43 *p. 266*]. This was particularly appealing in an age when Macmillan's Edwardian hauteur was looking increasingly anachronistic. 'My tastes are simple,' Wilson claimed in an interview. 'If I had the choice between smoked salmon and tinned salmon I'd have it tinned. With vinegar' [43 *p. 267*]. He was also successful in projecting an image of the Labour Party as modern, dynamic and progressive. In his speech to the Labour Party Conference at Scarborough in October 1963 he stressed Labour's commitment to science and technology as the means to build a more successful future [*Doc. 10*]. This appealed to the left of the party because it implied a welcome emphasis on planning; it appealed to the Gaitskellite revisionists because he appeared to be abandoning the 'outdated' commitment to nationalisation. To his audience he seemed to have succeeded in 'bringing together the disparate strands of post-war radical thinking into a cohesive and inspiring new doctrine' [43 *p. 305*].

Wilson also successfully exploited the government's growing economic difficulties, and handled Labour's response to the Profumo Affair with skill and restraint. Labour's lead in the opinion polls was sustained and extended, and the party looked forward to the coming election with high hopes. In the event, the election of 1964 was won with an overall majority of just five seats. However, it was still a remarkable victory, since the Labour Party had achieved the largest swing since 1945. Its days of division and the threat of perpetual opposition appeared to be over.

THE LIBERAL PARTY: DECLINE AND REVIVAL

In the early 1950s the Liberal Party seemed to be on the verge of extinction. Short of funds, it lacked a distinctive philosophy or a natural constituency. The leader, Clement Davies, was elderly and ineffective, and the party could not decide whether it was a left-of-centre alternative to Labour or a middle-class rival of the Conservatives. Its MPs gave conflicting advice to potential supporters who had no Liberal candidate to vote for. In each of the elections of 1951 and 1955 the party contested only a little over 100 constituencies, and nearly two-thirds of its candidates lost their deposits. Receiving less than 3 per cent of the votes, the party won a meagre six seats in each election. It could not even manage a united front over the Suez Crisis.

In the second half of the decade its fortunes improved. From 1956 Jo Grimond provided vigorous leadership, and a by-election victory in 1958 was followed by a more respectable general election result in 1959 in which the Liberal share of the vote doubled, even though the party still won only six seats. In 1962, as middle-class voters became disenchanted with Macmillan's government, the Liberals achieved a spectacular by-election success in Orpington, turning a Tory majority of 14,760 into a Liberal one of 7,855. There was much talk of a Liberal revival and one newspaper opinion poll even put them ahead of the Tories and Labour [57]. Subsequent by-elections, and the municipal elections of May 1962, suggested that the Liberals had become, once again, an important third force in British politics. The party's morale, finances and publicity all benefited.

However, before long the revival began to evaporate. The successes of 1962 had all been won at the expense of the Conservatives, and by the end of 1963 the opinion polls and by-elections were showing a return to two-party domination. Nevertheless, the party entered the 1964 election in good spirits. It fielded 365 candidates and Grimond fought a successful, high-profile campaign. The results, however, were mixed and established the pattern of Liberal fortunes ever since. Although the Liberal popular vote topped three million and contributed to the defeat of the government, the party won only nine constituencies because the electoral system prevented it from turning a solid core of popular support into parliamentary seats. It was also clear that the more spectacular Liberal successes like Orpington had had less to do with the party's intrinsic merits than with disenchanted Tory voters registering a protest against an unpopular government.

PART TWO: ANALYSIS

2 MANAGING THE ECONOMY

BUTSKELLISM

Analysis of Britain's economic performance in the 1950s is still dominated by the figure of 'Mr Butskell', who was invented in February 1954 by *The Economist* from the names of R.A. Butler and Hugh Gaitskell to suggest that the economic policies of the Conservative government were essentially the same as those of the previous Labour administrations [*Doc. 11*]. The name has stuck because there existed a considerable measure of agreement between the two main parties about economic goals and how to achieve them. Many historians [5; 17; 61; 65] believe that this consensus extended to most other areas of government policy.

Economic thinking in the 1950s was influenced by the ideas of John Maynard Keynes (1883–1946), who had challenged the orthodox economics of the 1930s by arguing that supply followed demand rather than the other way round. According to Keynes, the budget, far from being a neutral statement of expenditure and revenue, was a potent weapon with which to manage the economy, as decisions about taxation and expenditure (known as fiscal policy) could be used to boost or limit demand. The experience of the Second World War made Keynes's ideas acceptable in government circles: they demonstrated how fiscal policy could be used successfully to control inflation in a period of near full employment. Keynes's ideas were the new orthodoxy – he appeared to offer post-war governments a way of managing the economy to secure full employment and low inflation while avoiding the rigours of a Stalinist command economy or the high levels of unemployment associated with the 1930s and the economics of pre-Keynesian capitalism. In 1938 Harold Macmillan, a disciple of Keynes, published a book called *The Middle Way* which openly acknowledged his influence, but it was unacceptable at that time to fellow Conservatives. Even his family nanny remarked, 'Mr Harold is a dangerous Pink' [32 *p. 109*]. But defeat in the 1945 election forced the Conservatives to rethink their economic policies. By 1951, they had accepted that it should be a principal aim of government to maintain full employment. This would have to be done by the Keynesian method of stimulating demand in times of recession by cutting taxation and increasing government expenditure. Similarly, budgetary controls could be applied to check inflation in times of boom by raising taxes or trimming spending plans. This explains why the policies followed by the Tories between 1951 and 1964 have been called 'Stop-Go'.

The notion of consensus on economic policy can be pushed too far; there remained significant differences between the two main parties. The Tories of the 1950s were much more inclined to use monetary policy (changes in the interest rate) as a weapon against inflation than Labour had been. Between 1945 and 1951 the bank rate (which today would be called the minimum lending rate) remained at 2 per cent, while under the Tories it fluctuated between 2 and 7 per cent. The Tories also wanted to reduce the standard rate of income tax, which under Labour had only come down from the wartime rate of 10 shillings (50p) in the pound to 9 shillings (45p) in 1951. They believed that low taxes were necessary to give people the incentive to earn and spend. Some differences, though, were more to do with rhetoric than substance. Conservative propaganda in the 1951 election stressed the determination to rid the economy of socialist 'controls' (subsidies, rationing and the extension of nationalisation), even though the Labour government had itself begun to dismantle some that had been imposed during the period of post-war austerity. Furthermore, the governments of the 1950s continued to invest heavily in the nationalised industries and to provide subsidies for agriculture. In the early 1960s, they even became converts to the kind of planning that had influenced government thinking in the 1940s.

Some historians [52; 78; 82] have questioned how far the theories of Keynes were fully adopted by government policy-makers, but it seems clear that both ministers and Treasury officials accepted at least two Keynesian precepts. These were that the maintenance of full employment should be a central aim of government policy and that fiscal policy could and should exert a powerful influence on the economy. But neither Labour nor Conservative governments were prepared to risk creating budget deficits to boost employment in times of recession [82]. It can be argued, of course, that with employment high throughout the 1950s governments did not need to contemplate running a budget deficit. Instead, the government's principal aims were to maintain the value of sterling by keeping inflation under control and to maintain the value of the pound as an international currency. This meant that policy was shaped more by the needs of the moment than by coherent employment or investment strategies. Whenever a balance-of-payments crisis loomed, or sterling came under pressure on the foreign exchanges, or domestic inflation showed signs of increasing too fast, the government imposed a period of 'Stop' in which spending was cut, taxes increased and/or interest rates pushed up. Once the economic indicators had improved, or an election loomed, policy was relaxed in a period of reflation or 'Go'.

BUTLER AT THE TREASURY

When the Conservatives took office in 1951 the country was beginning to emerge from a period of austerity essential to its economic recovery from the Second World War. The Labour governments of 1945–51 had succeeded in boosting Britain's exports, restricting consumer demand and persuading the trade unions to accept wage restraint. These policies, together with the benefits of Marshall Aid and the increased liberalisation of world trade, helped to fulfil the prophecy that Keynes had made in a memorandum to the Cabinet in August 1945: 'Beyond question we are entering into the age of abundance'. The immediate prospects facing the new Chancellor were, however, bleak [*Doc. 12*]. The outbreak of the Korean War in 1950 had turned Britain's balance of payments from a £300m surplus in 1950 to a £400m deficit in 1951 [60], as the price of raw materials rose and rearmament increased Britain's import bill. The situation was worsened by speculation against the pound caused by international dealers' scepticism about Britain's capacity to cope with the crisis. Butler's task at the Treasury was not helped by Churchill's eccentric appointment of the elderly Sir Arthur Salter to the newly created post of Minister of State for Economic Affairs. Churchill commended him to Butler as 'the best economist since Jesus Christ' [21 *p. 156*]. As Butler laconically observes in his memoirs, Salter achieved nothing more than 'numberless minutes in green ink, with which I did not always agree' [21 *p. 156*]. Salter was also politically ineffective, and the Chancellor ignored him [34].

Butler reacted to the crisis he had inherited by imposing a series of cuts to reduce the import bill by £600m. These included restricting the amount that tourists could take abroad at any one time to £25 [60]. Butler's measures set the tone for Conservative economic policy in the 1950s. The needs of the moment rather than coherent philosophy determined decisions. Having denounced socialist control in its electoral campaign, the new government began its life by imposing some controls of its own. Butler also raised the bank rate by what now seems a modest 0.5 per cent, although it was regarded as significant at the time because it was the first change since before the war. It was raised again to 4 per cent in his first budget. Early in 1952 he imposed some hire-purchase restrictions but was able to introduce a neutral budget in March because domestic demand had already been dampened by Gaitskell's tax increases, the impact of high import prices and the concentration on rearmament. The 1952 budget cut government spending on food subsidies and reduced income tax, but increased the tax on petrol, leaving the consumer's purchasing power largely unchanged.

The clash between Conservative free-market ideals and the constraints imposed by prevailing conditions is also illustrated by the failure in February 1952 of the incongruously named 'Operation Robot'. The name derived from the initials of the Bank of England officials who conceived the scheme. They were concerned about the drain on Britain's reserves caused by the fixed exchange rate: the market value of the pound fell if foreigners lost confidence in it or if Britain's exports were doing badly. While the exchange rate remained fixed, the Bank of England was forced to buy pounds from those wishing to sell them at a rate higher than that of the markets. The result was a drain on the reserves which, if it worsened, could turn into a crisis similar to that of 1931. Robot proposed that the pound should 'float', with its value determined by the markets. This, of course, amounted to devaluation, which would have serious consequences for the countries, many of them in the Commonwealth, who made up the 'Sterling Area' and used the pound for their international trade. Their foreign-currency earnings, as well as Britain's, would be reduced by devaluation. Aware of this danger, the authors of Robot hedged it round with limitations, but it was still too radical for the Cabinet, who were worried not only by the potential hostility of the Commonwealth but also about the possibility of increased inflation and unemployment if the pound sank in value. Butler received scant support in the Cabinet and the scheme was dropped. As Kenneth Morgan has observed: 'A party devoted to decontrol and encouraging the private market, decided firmly in favour of control and management' [17 *p. 122*].

Butler later regretted the defeat of Robot, writing in his memoirs that 'the decision not to free the pound was a fundamental mistake. . . . Conservatives would have been saved some of the uncertainties and indignities of "stop-go" economics' [21 *p. 158*]. Such a claim can be treated with scepticism. Stop-Go policies were a response to the failure of the British economy in the 1950s to achieve sustained growth without inflation which Britain's major competitors seemed able to do, and freeing the pound was unlikely to have done much to assist Britain's competitive position. It was not until 1958 that the government felt strong enough to allow sterling to become fully convertible. A floating pound had to wait until 1972.

During 1952, Britain's balance of payments improved dramatically. This was due to the falling cost of imports as the terms of trade turned in Britain's favour, and to the recession in consumer demand which had begun before Butler took office. The government, naturally enough, attributed the improvement to Butler's monetary measures. It is more likely that his policies worsened the situation, as the improvement was under way before they took effect, so that his higher interest rates slowed growth and investment just when they needed to expand. The Conservatives in the 1950s were often to find that, by the time a problem had been diagnosed, statistics gathered and policies implemented, the worst of the crisis had passed. Stop-Go, instead of working against the economic cycle as it should have done, sometimes reinforced it.

By April 1953, Butler felt confident enough about the recovery to introduce an expansionary budget. Income tax was cut by 6d (2½p) in the pound and purchase tax (the forerunner of VAT) by 1s 6d (7½p). Economic recovery also enabled the government to end rationing, beginning with tea in October 1952, and going on to sugar, sweets, cream and eggs in 1953, and butter, cheese, margarine, cooking fats and meat in 1954. Churchill was keen to end rationing because it fulfilled an election pledge to abolish the Labour government's economic controls and would undoubtedly be popular. The drop in import prices ensured that the easing of rationing did not produce a sudden rise in the price of food, fear of which clearly influenced some members of the government who were worried about ending rationing too quickly [79].

In 1954, Butler and his Treasury advisers could not make up their minds whether the recession they feared to be imminent in the United States would hit Britain's exports or whether further economic expansion in Britain would cause inflation. The result was a neutral budget. The only innovation was an allowance designed to encourage investment in industry. Lord Woolton, the Party Chairman, confided to his diary that the budget was 'the dullest thing that anybody ever created' [79 *p. 174*]. As J.C.R. Dow has written: 'Bugetary policy thus still trod its perpetual compromise between the desire for more expansion and the fear of too much' [60 *p. 76*].

Butler, however, was making grand claims for the achievements of the government. In a speech in Gloucester on 10 July 1954 he said: 'In the past three years we have burned our identity cards, torn up our ration books . . . and said good riddance to nearly two-thirds of the remaining wartime regulations' [21 *p. 173*]. Others were more sceptical about these claims of Conservative radicalism, as the creation of the character of Mr Butskell shows. Butler also anticipated an exciting future. As his fears of an American recession receded, he promised the Party Conference of October 1954 that Tories would double the standard of living in Britain in 25 years. Even as this prediction was being made, it was clear to the Chancellor and his advisers that the boom was leading to a sizable increase in Britain's import bill. Early in 1955 the balance of payments was in deficit and inflation was accelerating. Butler applied the brakes by increasing the bank rate twice and re-introducing restrictions on hire-purchase agreements. The budget in April might reasonably have been expected to continue this deflationary trend, but Butler was to claim that his monetary policies had worked and that the economic situation allowed him to cut income tax by 6d (2½p) and reduce the tax on a pint of beer by 2d. His tax cuts amounted to more than £130m. This was a shamelessly electioneering budget. Churchill had at last retired and it was clear that the new Prime Minister, Anthony Eden, would want a general election as soon as possible. Anthony Seldon exonerates Butler, claiming that he 'should not be blamed too heavily for the April 1955 miscalculation' [79 *p. 176*]. He argues that the Chancellor was given conflicting advice and was under pressure from Tory backbenchers not to produce another damp squib like the 1954 budget. However, most commentators (including Butler's biographer) are closer to Kenneth Morgan's verdict that Butler had 'imperilled the finances in his budget for purely electioneering purposes' [17 *p. 123*; 81].

With the election over and the government's majority increased, Butler was forced to repent his budget decisions as the inflationary pressures mounted. During the summer of 1955 the banks were told to restrict credit and there were further restrictions on hire purchase. None of this was enough and, when the pound came under pressure, Butler introduced a supplementary budget in October in which he increased purchase tax by one-fifth and applied it to previously exempt items such as kitchen utensils. This won it the title of the 'pots and pans' budget. Gaitskell launched a furious assault on Butler in the Commons, accusing him of deliberate deceit. 'Having bought his votes with a bribe, the Chancellor is forced – as he knew he would be – to dishonour the cheque. . . . He has behaved in a manner unworthy of his high office. He began in folly, he continued in deceit, and he has ended in reaction' [4, 545 *col. 408*]. Butler also lacked the full support of his Prime Minister, who was already planning to replace him with Macmillan. Eden's memoirs make it clear that he found the budget measures distasteful: 'These decisions were thought economically right at the time, they were certainly politically odious and cut across our party's philosophy. It is difficult to advocate a property-owning democracy to the tune of "Your kettles will cost more" ' [27 *p. 316*].

MACMILLAN AT No. 11 AND No. 10

In December Butler became Leader of the House of Commons and Macmillan took over at the Treasury. In his memoirs Butler ruefully admits that he might have resigned earlier and that it would have been better for his reputation if he had: 'If I had been less scrupulous about the economy I would have retired in May' [21 *p. 180*]. His four-year stewardship of the Treasury has not been treated generously by historians, despite the fact that for three years at least it looked as if he had produced a golden age of low inflation, full employment, steady growth and balance-of-payments surpluses. Most historians believe that the improvement in Britain's economic fortunes between 1951 and 1954 owed more to world conditions than to Tory policies. It was improvement in Britain's terms of trade and the stimulus to recovery caused by the ending of the Korean War that enabled wartime restrictions such as rationing to be removed. The prosperity from which the Conservatives benefited electorally in 1955 was not the product of their policies; it enabled them to liberalise their policies and claim credit for what would have occurred anyway. Butler and his colleagues had demonstrated that they could employ controls just as vigorously as their Labour predecessors when the economic situation seemed to demand them, as Butler's response to the 1951 crisis and the failure of Robot demonstrate. Butler has also been criticised for indecision. Macmillan, admittedly not an impartial source, called him 'protean' and a man 'who does not appear to have any views on anything himself' [*32 p. 378*]. Butler, lacking any background in economics, certainly relied heavily on the advice he received from his Treasury and Bank of England advisers, which was not always consistent. It is difficult to identify any very clear-cut economic principles to which he was committed, and, if the political opposition was strong, he seemed ever willing to retreat from policies based on conviction, such as Operation Robot. M. Pinto-Duschinsky, anticipating 1980s Thatcherite criticism of the Tories of the 1950s, regards Butler's 1955 budget as 'the turning-point . . . in the whole post-war economy' [*9 p. 64*] because it began the inflationary spiral that was to bedevil the British economy for the next two decades: 'Had the inflationary strains been eased during 1955, it would probably have been possible to maintain the stability of prices and to continue to produce the growth rates that had been achieved in 1953 and 1954. Stop-Go would in that case not have gained its momentum' [*9 p. 68*]. Butler receives a more generous, if not effusive, assessment from Anthony Seldon: 'Butler inherited a favourable position, which he had the good sense not to waste' [*79 p. 178*]. Perhaps it is illustrative of his career as Chancellor that he is best remembered for his part as one-half of the economic pantomime horse: Mr Butskell.

Macmillan, the new Chancellor, began his tenure full of reforming zeal, enthusing about convertibility and cutting food subsidies, but the gravity of the inflationary crisis prevented the former and he met opposition to the latter from the Prime Minister. However, he succeeded in overcoming Eden's objections and introduced further deflationary measures by raising the bank rate, cutting investment programmes and tightening the restrictions on hire purchase. By the time Macmillan presented his only budget in April 1956, he felt confident that the crisis was under control and raised taxes only modestly. As an incentive to save, he introduced Premium Bonds, which his opposition counterpart, Harold Wilson, immediately denounced as 'a squalid raffle' [*4, 551 col. 1026*].

The Suez Crisis of 1956 brought further economic troubles, as the pound came under severe pressure on the international exchanges. The Bank of England lost $84m during October and a further $50m in the first two days of November, once the Anglo-French assault on Egypt had begun. Nasser's retaliatory action of blocking the canal prevented Britain from receiving oil supplies. When the Americans made it clear that an International Monetary Fund (IMF) loan to shore up the pound and enable Britain to buy oil was dependent on a cease-fire, Britain's Suez adventure had, in effect, been ended by

American financial power [115]. The impact of the Suez Crisis on the domestic economy, however, was limited to a temporary rationing of petrol.

Suez made Macmillan Prime Minister, and he appointed Peter Thorneycroft as his Chancellor. By the time of his budget in April 1957 the economy had been subjected to a year and a half of deflationary measures. Thorneycroft decided that it was time for a period of 'Go', announcing in his budget speech that 'expansion must be the theme' [4, 568 *col. 982*]. The effect of his measures was to reduce taxation by £100m, but it was not long before he was assailed with worries about inflation. In August 1957 the devaluation of the French franc started a wave of speculation against the pound, as speculators wrongly believed that Britain was about to abandon its fixed exchange rate and allow the pound to float. This convinced Thorneycroft that the thrust of his budget had been misguided and that a further dose of deflation was necessary. In September 1957 he raised the bank rate by 2 per cent to an unprecedented 7 per cent. On 29 October Thorneycroft outlined to Parliament the policies he intended to follow [*Doc. 13*]. In July he had established a three-man Council on Prices, Productivity and Incomes (immediately nicknamed 'the three wise men') which endorsed his policies and was, accordingly, boycotted by the Trades Union Congress and caustically dismissed by the Shadow Chancellor as 'the appointment of three distinguished elderly gentlemen to prepare sermons to be addressed to the trade unions' [4, 575 *col. 62*]. Macmillan did not share Thorneycroft's monetarist principles, regarding them as reminiscent of Chamberlain's rigid and insensitive economic orthodoxy. In January 1958 the two men clashed and Thorneycroft resigned, along with his Treasury ministers, Enoch Powell and Nigel Birch. What was apparently at issue was a relatively trivial increase in government expenditure, but the real cause went to the heart of economic policy. For Macmillan, the main danger was recession and he was prepared to risk mild inflation to achieve full employment. Thorneycroft and his Treasury colleagues regarded the maintenance of price stability as paramount and they were prepared to risk rising unemployment to achieve it. Thorneycroft's resignation meant that, when monetarism became fashionable in the 1980s, he was regarded as a John the Baptist figure whose political defeat had signalled the start of Britain's inflationary decline.

The new Chancellor was Derick Heathcoat Amory, who in April 1958 introduced a mildly inflationary budget in which tax cuts of

£50m were announced. Both Amory and Macmillan were worried that recession in the United States might affect employment in Britain. During the summer the government relaxed the controls on bank credit and hire purchase. These measures helped to stimulate demand and output in Britain but did not upset the balance of payments, as Britain's import bill fell during 1958 due to a decline in world commodity prices. Unemployment in Britain had been rising in 1958, so Amory, with a little prodding from Macmillan, produced an expansionary budget in 1959. In his budget speech, Amory pointed out that there had been a rise in production and demand, but added: 'this rise is not likely to be at all rapid – indeed, if nothing more were done, it might slow down in the second half of the year' [4, 603 *col. 44*]. The fear of imminent recession, and the electoral advantage to be gained from a generous budget, explain the extent of the cuts. Purchase tax was reduced by 1s 6d (7½p), income tax from 8s 6d (42½p) in the pound to 7s 9d (39p), the tax on beer came down and investment allowances were restored. The budget contributed to the Tories' third consecutive electoral triumph in October. Furthermore, as the expected recession did not materialise, the economy expanded in 1959. Output, production and demand all rose and unemployment fell. Early in 1960, however, all the usual worrying signs accompanying a boom began to appear. The balance-of-payments surpluses began to fall because consumer demand was sucking in imports, and prices and wages were edging upwards. In February 1960 Macmillan had authorised a 5 per cent wage increase for the railwaymen, in order to avoid a strike, and this concession was likely to be followed by demands from other workers. Macmillan was determined to resist the demands for severe deflation, and in a letter to Amory on 27 February he requested a 'stand-still budget' and lamented the cycle of Stop-Go policies which he characterised in distinctively wry fashion: 'The new Progressive Conservatism will turn out to be a policy of alternation between Benzadrine and Relaxa-tabs. I don't like it at all' [33 *p. 238*]. Amory, like Butler before him, tried to use monetary measures to cool the overheating. In January the bank rate had been increased, and it was raised again in June, while in April hire-purchase restrictions were tightened. Amory's 1960 budget was neutral as far as consumers' spending power was concerned, although it increased the profits tax to 12.5 per cent to bring the Exchequer an extra £72m a year [19; 60]. Amory had never felt entirely at ease with the reflationary policies he had implemented in 1959, and as early as May of that year he told Macmillan that he wanted to retire after the election, anticipating that he and the Prime Minister would disagree about economic policy before long. It was no surprise when Amory was replaced by Selwyn Lloyd in July 1960.

Selwyn Lloyd, writes Alistair Horne, was 'Macmillan's least successful appointment' [33 *p. 245*]. He has generally been regarded as a loyal and hard-working minister who lacked the independence and vision necessary for either of the two principal offices he held. Peter Clarke calls him 'the perfect team-player, a competent utility man who wanted to fit in but displayed no obvious ambition or capacity to take over as captain' [56 *p. 220*]. Nevertheless, he shared both Macmillan's liberal economic philosophy and his faith in economic planning, and was thus more in sympathy with the Prime Minister than either of the two previous Chancellors had been.

Lloyd inherited a difficult legacy. Britain's export performance, despite the boom, was poor by comparison with her major competitors, and this threatened the balance of payments. Consumer spending and wage costs were pushing inflation higher and the government was faced with a number of strikes and threatened strikes during 1960. Although Lloyd felt confident enough to reduce the bank rate twice during the autumn of 1960, his preparations for his first budget were affected by a sudden run on the pound in March 1961. This was triggered by the revaluation of the German mark and reflected the loss of confidence of the money markets in Britain's balance of payments and economic prospects. Temporary relief came from an agreement reached in Basle by which a number of continental Central Banks bought sterling [47; 53]. Lloyd's budget, introduced in April 1961, was concerned principally with restraining consumer demand, and he returned to fiscal measures as his main instruments for doing so. Although he increased the amount that people could earn before paying surtax, he also raised profits tax and made motoring more expensive. The main innovation was the introduction of 'regulators' which would allow a Chancellor to alter the level of some taxes and contributions without recourse to a budget. This was only a mildly deflationary budget and it was not enough to stave off a further crisis in the summer.

As the trade figures worsened and pressure on the pound continued, Lloyd was forced to introduce his 'little budget' on 25 July. This provided a more drastic dose of deflation. The bank rate was raised to 7 per cent, credit squeezed, indirect taxes increased and public expenditure cut. These measures enabled the government to secure a large IMF loan, and by August the worst of the sterling crisis was over. Lloyd has not escaped criticism, however, and to

Samuel Brittan his measures are another example of the Tories applying the medicine too late and hindering recovery. 'By the time the Chancellor acted, the underlying balance of payments was satisfactory and rapidly improving – a fact which was apparent at the time from the trade figures . . . the economy was in any case coming off the boil and the Chancellor simply made sure that an easing of business activity turned into a recession' [*53 p. 231*].

The July budget heralded a further innovation in Conservative economic management. In explaining that the previous year had seen an 8 per cent increase in incomes but only a 3 per cent increase in production, Lloyd claimed that a 'pay pause' in the public sector was necessary. This ran into immediate trouble: wage restraint was imposed on workers such as nurses and teachers whose industrial muscle was weak, but for whom there was considerable public sympathy, while the credibility of the pay pause was seriously damaged by the increase granted to the electricity workers in November.

Despite these difficulties, Macmillan and Lloyd pressed ahead with another project which appealed to their instincts for interventionist policies and economic planning. The government created the National Economic Development Council (or NEDC, popularly known as 'Neddy'), which comprised representatives from government, management and unions. Its tasks were to review the economic prospects of the nation, identify problems and suggest ways of promoting faster economic growth [*Doc. 14*]. Enthusiasm for such an initiative owed something to the belief that the French had achieved economic success as a result of planning; even the Federation of British Industries was willing to extend planning to the private sector. However, such ideas were at odds with the traditional Tory free-market philosophy, as critics within the Cabinet and party did not fail to point out. The Conservative journalist, Henry Fairlie, wrote in the September 1962 edition of *Encounter* that the creation of Neddy represented 'almost the exact reverse of the attitude of "Set the People Free", which was Conservatism in 1951; of "Conservative Freedom Works", which became Conservatism before and after 1955, and of "I'm all right, Jack", which was Conservatism in 1959' [*10 p. 139*].

As he prepared his second budget in 1962, Selwyn Lloyd could reasonably claim to be an innovative Chancellor. His first budget had attempted reform of the taxation system, and he aimed to do more in the future to reduce the burden of direct taxation [47]. With the formation of the NEDC, which held its first meeting in March 1962, he had also taken a major step towards consensus planning of Britain's economic future. Although his 1961 pay pause had met immediate opposition, it may have contributed to a temporary slowing in the inflation rate. Lloyd had also been able to reduce the bank rate to 6 per cent in the autumn, as the economy appeared to be cooling. He pressed on with his incomes policy and in February 1962 announced a 2.5 per cent 'guiding light' for pay increases. This provoked strikes by railwaymen, postmen and nurses and was ignored by the private sector. Opposition to it and the need for a more dramatic policy led Macmillan to take the initiative by forming the National Incomes Commission (or NIC, soon to be known as 'Nicky'), which came into being in July 1962 with the purpose of reviewing wage claims in the light of the national interest. Although Nicky lacked any statutory power, the unions were implacably opposed to anything that smacked of an incomes policy and refused to participate.

Lloyd's 1962 budget was economically neutral but politically unsuccessful. It abolished a tax on privately owned houses and introduced one on short-term capital gains that was designed to reduce speculation in stocks and shares. At the time, its most notable feature was a 15 per cent tax on sweets. It was hardly a budget to revive the Conservatives' flagging political fortunes, nor did it seem to suggest a dynamic sense of vision about how Britain was to achieve sustained economic growth without repeated inflationary crises. However, in July 1962 Selwyn Lloyd was surprised and shocked to be sacked in the 'Night of the Long Knives'; a victim of Macmillan's political anxiety rather than any economic failure on his own part [51].

The new Chancellor was the 45-year-old Reginald Maudling. He was appointed because he was a young, buoyant personality and because, as Samuel Brittan has written, Macmillan 'wanted above all someone who could understand economic policy and was able to express himself on the subject in public' [53 p. 249]. The task facing Maudling was a difficult one. The government was still committed to an incomes policy, because it feared the inflationary effects of wage rises. However, with Lloyd's pay pause a political millstone, strikes continuing and the unions refusing to cooperate with Nicky, the policy was proving hard to sustain. Furthermore, there were fears of a renewed slump. Britain was entering a period of 'stagflation' (slow growth and stubbornly high levels of unemployment combined with rising inflation) which belied the optimistic nostrums of Keynes's devotees. Before he left office, Lloyd had been planning a dose of reflation, after receiving a forecast from the Ministry of Labour that unemployment would exceed 500,000 in the forthcoming winter. To a government still wedded to the notion of full employment, such a figure was politically damaging.

In his Mansion House speech in October 1962, the new Chancellor announced a small package of measures to expand the economy: an increase in public investment and the ending of the credit squeeze. Maudling also reduced the burden of purchase tax in two stages (as Lloyd's 1961 regulator allowed him to do), but the total cuts amounted only to about £90m. Macmillan wanted a much more radical approach. In November 1962 he prepared a memorandum in which he demanded an increase in productivity 'to enhance our competitive power and to ensure a level of exports commensurate with full employment at home' and measures 'to rectify the imbalance between . . . the over-employed regions and the under-employed regions' [33 *p. 469*]. In pursuit of this latter objective, in January 1963 he appointed the flamboyant Lord Hailsham to be minister with special responsibility for the North-East, and in October he created a new Ministry of Industry, Trade and Regional Development headed by Edward Heath. Macmillan still believed that benevolently managed capitalism could alleviate the plight of the unemployed, as he had articulated in the *The Middle Way* in the 1930s.

The severity of the 1962–63 winter, with its impact on production, and the failure of Britain's application to join the EEC in January 1963, lent a new urgency to the economic situation. Macmillan had backed the application to Europe not only to boost his flagging political prestige, but also to supply Britain with access to expanding European markets and provide a stimulus for modernisation. Maudling, fortified by a Neddy report in February 1963 setting a 4 per cent annual growth target for the British economy, prepared an expansionary budget. 'Maudling's measures amounted to the biggest level of tax relief since Hugh Dalton in Labour's high noon after 1945' [17 *p. 213*]. His tax cuts totalled nearly £300m, and there were incentives for industrial investment and plans for expanded public investment, especially in the depressed areas of the North, Scotland and Wales, where unemployment levels were of particular concern.

By the end of the year it seemed that Maudling's policies were working. Exports rose, unemployment fell and productivity was increasing. Nevertheless, Maudling was forced to continue with an incomes policy to avoid rampant inflation, although Selwyn Lloyd's 2.5 per cent guiding light had been expanded to 3–3.5 per cent. The signs of strain made themselves clear in the worsening balance-of-payments figures. Maudling had hoped that by expanding production and boosting investment he would improve Britain's export performance and thus achieve growth without a balance-of-payments deficit. Like many subsequent Chancellors, he was to find that when the British economy is expanded, consumer spending, which sucks in imports, rises faster than export production. By the time of the general election in October 1964, Britain's trade gap was £800m, giving the Labour Party a potent weapon with which to criticise Conservative stewardship of the economy.

Labour won the election, but the closeness of the result clearly owed something to the renewed sense of consumer prosperity that Maudling's pursuit of growth had generated. Nevertheless, the Conservatives' 13-year reign ended with a distinct impression that, once again, short-term electoral advantage had prevailed over economic wisdom. Labour's new Chancellor, Jim Callaghan, recalls arriving at 11 Downing Street and finding Maudling busy packing in the upstairs flat. Maudling apologised: 'Sorry, old cock, to leave it in this shape' [22 *p. 162*]. Doubtless he was referring to the state of the flat, but the remark could also be seen as a verdict on his tenure at the Treasury.

3 FOREIGN POLICY

DELUSIONS OF GRANDEUR

'Britain is going to continue to be what she has been, a Great Power' [45 *p. 104*], declared the 1954 Reith Lecturer. Oliver Franks, who had recently returned from a spell as Britain's ambassador in Washington, was stating no more than was commonly believed at the time. Nor was this an idle conceit. In 1950 Britain produced a quarter of the world's manufacturing exports – more than France, Germany and Japan put together, and only marginally less than the Americans [52]. She controlled a vast colonial empire in the Middle East, Africa and the Far East. British forces were engaged in the Korean War, and in fighting the insurgents in Malaya, two divisions were stationed in Germany, and there were sizable units in the Middle East, Hong Kong, Trieste and Kenya. Altogether, nearly one million men were under arms [93]. As a permanent member of the Security Council of the United Nations and the proud owner of an independent nuclear deterrent, Britain could still claim to be a major world power and America's principal partner in NATO. British leaders believed that a special relationship existed with the United States, based on Britain's unique role in what Churchill called the 'three great circles among the free nations and democracies'. By this he meant the English-speaking world of Britain and America, the Commonwealth and Europe. Since Britain was 'the only country which has a great part in every one of them' [124 *p. 202*] he argued that her influence in each was enhanced by her role in the other two.

Events were to demonstrate that this theory was little more than a comforting illusion, yet in 1950 Churchill's notion had some merit. Britain had been one of the architects of NATO and, as such, had played a key role in persuading the Americans to abandon their traditional policy of isolation and commit themselves in peacetime to the defence of Europe. Despite the granting of independence to

India in 1947 and Palestine in 1948, there was not much thought of dissolving the Empire any further. Indeed, policy-makers hoped to tie the colonies more closely to Britain by controlling their economic development. Britain's informal empire in the Middle East – her network of client states in the area – assumed greater significance in the early 1950s because of the importance of the region's oil, its proximity to the Soviet Union and its geographical position as the link between the two non-communist areas of the Far East and the North Atlantic. Britain had also played a leading role in coordinating Europe's response to Marshall Aid. Even as late as 1957, Macmillan claimed that Britain was the leading European power.

Although it was painfully clear in the early 1950s that Britain's overseas commitments exceeded her capacity to sustain them, this was not a new problem; it had been Britain's principal foreign-policy headache since the beginning of the century. Solving it was more difficult in the post-war years because the facts of Britain's diminished status became ever starker. The solution which recommended itself to the new Conservative government was outlined by Foreign Secretary Eden in a Cabinet paper of June 1952. Britain should try to create a series of international defence organisations and 'persuade the United States to assume the real burdens in such organisations while retaining for ourselves as much political control – and hence prestige and world influence – as we can' [Doc. 15]. This would enable Britain to exercise world power and influence on the cheap. Defence policy followed a similar logic. Nuclear weapons were assumed to be less expensive than large conventional forces, but would allow Britain to continue as a world power.

The problems with these assumptions were to become all too clear in the 1950s. The relationship with the United States raised two principal difficulties. First, although they welcomed Britain as an ally in the Cold War, the Americans retained their suspicion of British imperialism, which they believed only encouraged colonial nationalists to turn to communism. British governments resented this attitude, regarding it as nothing more than a cloak under which the Americans could substitute their influence for British. The second problem was that nuclear weapons did not turn out to be cheaper than conventional forces. Instead, economic weakness and the escalating costs of nuclear technology forced Britain into a position, not of partnership with the United States, but of dependence. British politicians also miscalculated their response to European economic integration. Believing that their ties with the Empire and Commonwealth were more important, the British adopted a lofty disdain towards the nascent EEC. By the time colonial nationalism had dissolved most of the Empire and Britain made a belated bid to join in 1961, she was left an importunate outsider. The 'political control . . . prestige and world influence' [*Doc. 15*] that in 1952 the Cabinet had hoped to exercise proved illusory.

EDEN AT THE FOREIGN OFFICE

When the Conservatives returned to office in 1951 it was inevitable that Anthony Eden would become Foreign Secretary. He had held the post twice before (1935–38 and 1940–45) and his knowledge and experience of foreign affairs were rivalled only by Churchill himself. The relationship between the two men during Churchill's final premiership was not, however, an easy or harmonious one. Eden fretted as Churchill tantalised him with promises that his retirement was imminent, only to renege on several occasions. Eden resented Churchill's interference in foreign affairs, partly because there were some serious policy differences between them and partly because both men were, as one Foreign Office official tartly commented, 'two-thirds prima donna' [26 p. 193].

Churchill's principal preoccupation during his premiership was his attempt, especially after Stalin's death in March 1953, to reconstruct the summit diplomacy of the war years. He believed that a meeting between himself, the US President and the new Soviet leadership could do much to reduce the tensions of the Cold War [132]. Churchill commended his idea to Parliament in May 1953 in characteristically emotive language: 'it might be that no hard-faced agreements would be reached, but there might be a general feeling among those gathered together that they might do something better than tear the human race, including themselves, into bits' [4, 515 col. 897]. Eden, however, was unenthusiastic. He felt that Churchill, neither sufficiently informed nor interested in diplomatic detail, might be tempted, with a grand wave of his post-prandial cigar, to concede too much of substance to the USSR. The Americans were also hostile to the idea. When Churchill discussed it with President Eisenhower in December 1953 and suggested that the USSR without Stalin was different, Eisenhower retorted that the USSR was like a whore who might have changed her clothes but still needed to be chased from the streets. Eisenhower's 1952 presidential campaign had castigated the Truman administration for being soft on communism, and at the time of Churchill's suggested summit, Senator McCarthy's anti-communist hysteria was at its height. It was hardly a suitable moment for Eisenhower to undertake anything that could be portrayed as appeasement of the USSR. Churchill's summit was destined never to take place, but while there was still even the smallest chance that it might, he continued to postpone his retirement. He was even contemplating doing so a mere nine days before he did finally hand over to Eden. When a four-power summit was held in Geneva in July 1955 it was, ironically, Eden who represented Britain; and although, according to Macmillan, the meeting was 'a great waste of time' [36 *p. 618*], the fact that it had occurred at all was taken as evidence that the Cold War was thawing a little. Perhaps Churchill's faith in summit diplomacy had achieved, albeit belatedly, a small measure of vindication.

Churchill and Eden also differed in their attitude to the United States. Eden disliked and distrusted the Americans, but realised that Britain could not do without them. He feared that American zeal for anti-communism might drag Britain and the rest of the world into war, or, paradoxically, that America might withdraw into a new period of isolation [45]. Churchill's attitude was simpler and was summed up in his parting advice to his junior ministers: 'Never be separated from the Americans' [30 *p. 1123*]. Eden's successor, Harold Macmillan, conducted British foreign policy as though Churchill's words were his lodestar.

Eden's uneasy relationship with the USA was apparent from his first days in office in dealing with two issues – Korea and Iran – inherited from the Labour government. The Korean War, which had begun in 1950, had reached stalemate by the spring of 1951 and armistice talks were started in the summer. True to its anti-communist credentials, the American government wanted its Western allies to support its tough stance. Eden was wary, because he feared that the Americans might provoke war with the Chinese. He also resented British exclusion from the newly created ANZUS Pact, by which Australia and New Zealand turned to the United States to guarantee their security. The pattern was thus set for Eden's attitude towards the Americans over the Far East: while reluctant to accept junior status, he sought to soften American anti-communism by adopting a more conciliatory policy.

In May 1951 the Prime Minister of Iran, Mohammed Mussadeq, had announced the nationalisation of the Anglo-Iranian Oil Company (AIOC, now known as BP). The Attlee government's response was muted, despite Morrison's initial belligerence, and the issue remained unresolved when Eden returned to the Foreign Office. The Americans had accepted Mussadeq's coup and were willing to offer him economic aid because they felt his government was strong enough to resist the Iranian communist party. Eden, who regarded Mussadeq as 'little more than a rug merchant' [25 *p. 307*] and a threat to Western interests, wanted him replaced with a more compliant regime which would restore the AIOC. According to his memoirs, Eden was even sanguine about the consequences for the West of a Soviet takeover in Iran. In January 1952 he persuaded the Americans not to provide aid to Iran until a joint policy had been agreed, and in August 1953 Mussadeq was overthrown in a coup supported by the CIA and British Intelligence. The Shah was returned to power and, in gratitude to his Western benefactors, maintained Iran as the principal pro-Western power in the region until his overthrow in 1979. The AIOC received compensation but lost its monopoly; Iranian oil wealth was now shared with the Americans. The episode is instructive because of its similarity to the Suez Crisis of 1956. Eden regarded Nasser as another 'rug merchant' to be dealt with in the same way. In both cases, the aim of British policy was to recover control of an important economic asset which had been seized by a nationalist leader, but was dressed up as the defence of international law and order. However, even Eden's sympathetic biographer is prepared to admit that British policy in the overthrow of Mussadeq 'is perhaps not for the pure in heart and soul' [35 *p. 360*].

In 1954 Eden achieved what many commentators regard as his finest hour: the Geneva Conference on Indo-China [132]. Since the 1860s Indo-China (which comprised what is now Vietnam, Laos and Cambodia) had been a French colony, but during the Second World War the Vichy regime in France had been forced to allow the Japanese to establish bases there. The Japanese were resisted by a nationalist movement in Vietnam called the Viet-Minh, led by Ho Chi Minh, who declared Vietnam independent in 1945. The French attempted to reassert their control and a vicious colonial war began. They established a puppet Vietnamese government in 1949 which was recognised by Britain and America, but in 1954 they requested American military help when it became clear that this was facing defeat at the hands of the Viet-Minh, who were now supported by the communist regime in China.

The imminent French collapse in Indo-China placed President Eisenhower in a dilemma. He regarded it as essential to contain the spread of international communism but was reluctant to commit American troops to another war like Korea. He did not want America to act alone, because this would seem like imperialism. So the Secretary of State, John Foster Dulles, attempted to create an anti-communist security pact, to be the Asian version of NATO, which would involve Britain, France, Australia, New Zealand and the nations of South-East Asia in joint resistance to communism. With the American Joint Chiefs of Staff contemplating US air strikes to assist the French, Eden was worried that Britain would be drawn into a conflict in the Far East. He was reluctant to commit himself to Dulles's security pact until after a peace conference, at which he hoped concessions could be made to the communists in order to achieve some stability in the region, had been held. Churchill gave Eden a free hand in these negotiations, remarking to one official that 'he had been able to remain ignorant about these areas all his life; it was hard that they had come to tease him in his old age' [25 p. 328].

Eden succeeded in convening the conference in Geneva in April 1954, attended by Britain, France, the USSR, America and China. Dulles was only reluctantly present and refused to shake hands with the leader of the Chinese delegation because America did not recognise the communist regime in Peking. After the fall of the main French garrison at Dien Bien Phu in May, the new French government, appointed in June, was anxious to withdraw from its hopeless position in Vietnam as quickly as possible. With the Soviets proving surprisingly conciliatory, an agreement was reached in July by which Vietnam was to be divided at the 17th Parallel and Laos and Cambodia were to become independent. The Americans felt let down by Eden because they believed Geneva had prevented a firm response to the spread of communism in Asia. When, in September, Dulles's security pact came into being as the South-East Asia Treaty Organisation (SEATO), it did no more than commit members to 'consult' about communist expansion [25]. Dulles believed that Eden had double-crossed him by promising that Britain would join SEATO before the Geneva Conference and then reneging on his promise in a statement to the House of Commons in April 1954.

Rhodes James argues that 'Eden, virtually single-handedly, had kept America out of a war in Indo-China that could easily have escalated into a major and appalling confrontation between the nuclear powers' [35 p. 380]. Not everyone saw it so at the time. To the Americans Eden was an appeaser; even the British satirical magazine *Punch* depicted him as a latter-day Chamberlain – a particularly ironic comment on a man whose reputation had been enhanced by his opposition to Chamberlain's appeasement of Italy. The Indo-China crisis, too, provides a curious mirror-image of the

Suez Crisis of 1956. In 1954 Eden resisted American demands for the concerted use of force against what the Americans perceived to be the spread of international communism; in 1956 he was to advocate the use of force against Nasser's Egypt (which he regarded as a communist surrogate) and was to find himself resisted by the Americans. Furthermore, the personal antipathy between Dulles and Eden that was to bedevil the diplomacy of 1956 probably dates from this crisis. Dulles felt cheated by Eden over Indo-China; in 1956 it was to be Eden who complained of similar treatment by Dulles.

Eden also played a significant part in 1954 in the resolution of the crisis over West German rearmament and in solving the dispute between Yugoslavia and Italy over Trieste. Since the war, the city, which was largely Italian in population, had been occupied by British and American troops. Yugoslavia had seized the hinterland, largely populated by Slavs, but this too was claimed by Italy. Eden, who in 1952 had been the first leading Western statesman to visit the Yugoslav leader Tito, was able to broker an agreement between Italy and Yugoslavia in October 1954 by which Italy annexed the city and Yugoslavia the hinterland.

Eden completed his 'annus mirabilis' of 1954 by negotiating a treaty which appeared to resolve Britain's troubled relationship with Egypt. Nominally independent since 1936, Egypt had effectively remained ruled by the British High Commissioner in Cairo. During the Second World War Britain had used Egypt as its main base in the Middle East, which meant that *de facto* British rule was restored. In 1947, in response to a request from the Egyptian government, British troops were withdrawn from Cairo and Alexandria to the Suez Canal Zone, where, under the terms of the 1936 treaty, the British were permitted to maintain a military base. Its future became a contentious issue. To successive British governments the maintenance of a secure base in the Middle East was essential to Britain's great-power status, not only in the region but around the world. Two principal factors complicated this. The first was American hostility to British imperialism in the Middle East, which the British regarded as sanctimonious cover for American ambitions in the area. The second problem was the strength of nationalist feeling in Egypt. This was particularly evident among the young officers of the Egyptian army, who blamed Britain for their defeat by Israel in the war of 1948–49. The British, for obvious reasons, had been reluctant to provide adequate weapons for an Egyptian army which disliked the presence of British troops in Egypt. As an embassy official reported to London in 1953: 'I believe that we are up against a determined anti-British movement. The young officers think we are on the decline as a great power, they have a real hatred politically for us in their hearts and they will accept assistance and guidance from any party or persons who will aid them in turning us completely out of Egypt. No amount of concession or evacuation on our part will evoke the slightest gratitude in return. Whoever Egypt may want in the future as an ally, it will not be us' [114 *pp. 412–13*].

British troops in the Canal Base found themselves subject to terrorist attacks, and there were serious anti-British riots in Cairo in January 1952. Eden, when he took over the Foreign Office in October 1951, recognised the need for Britain to withdraw from Egypt. He was aware that the Suez Canal Base was less important to Britain after Indian independence in 1947. He could also see the truth of Dalton's earlier observation about British rule in Palestine: 'you cannot have . . . a secure base on top of a wasp's nest' [124 *p. 186*]. British withdrawal was complicated by three factors. First, given Britain's network of client states in the Middle East and the importance of the area to Britain's view of her status, an alternative base would need to be found. Secondly, no British Foreign Secretary could sanction withdrawal while the Egyptian government claimed sovereignty over Sudan, to which Britain had promised self-determination. Thirdly, a small but vociferous group of Tory MPs, known as the Suez Group, were opposed to withdrawal from the base. Eden, in trying to negotiate with the Egyptians, found himself undermined by Churchill who encouraged the Suez Group [109; 118] and 'wrote them supportive letters whenever they attacked Eden' [44 *p. 787*].

The chances of an agreement were greatly improved when Egypt's corrupt monarchy was overthrown by a military coup in July 1952. The new regime, headed by Nasser, was prepared to abandon its claim to Sudan. This removed the remaining justification for retaining British troops in the Canal Base. The British government also took the decision to develop Cyprus as a military and air force base for 7,500 British service personnel [93], even though this would involve vast expenditure. With the Americans urging British withdrawal and the Chiefs of Staff supporting the idea, Eden was able to overcome Churchill's objections. By the treaty signed in October 1954 all British troops were to withdraw from the Canal Base by 18 June 1956, although they would be permitted to return if an Arab state or Turkey were attacked by an outside power other than Israel (i.e., the USSR). British civilian technicians were to remain at the base for seven years to maintain it. The Egyptians also endorsed the 1888 Convention which guaranteed freedom of navigation through the Suez Canal.

There were signs in 1955 that the Cold War in Europe was beginning to thaw a little. By the terms of the Austrian State Treaty signed in May, all occupying forces were to withdraw from Austria, which became fully independent and neutral. This was a breakthrough because, for the first time, communist forces had withdrawn voluntarily from an occupied territory. In July 1955 at Geneva, Eden achieved the summit conference that had eluded Churchill. Although it generated some optimism, known for a while afterwards as the 'spirit of Geneva', little of substance was agreed. The Soviet Union hoped that, following Austria's example, Germany might also be neutralised. This was unacceptable to the Western powers who had just achieved the admission of West Germany to NATO. There was also fruitless discussion of the vexed problem of arms limitation and verification. Eden did succeed in inviting the new Soviet leaders to visit London. Bulganin and Khrushchev arrived in April 1956 and, like the Geneva summit, their visit achieved little – apart from a feeling that the new generation of Soviet leaders were less terrifying than Stalin.

Of more long-term significance than these summits was a meeting in June 1955 at Messina. France, Italy, West Germany and the Benelux countries began the process that was to lead to the creation of the European Economic Community. These six countries had already achieved a significant degree of economic cooperation by creating the European Coal and Steel Community (ECSC) in 1952. Given the role that Britain had played in promoting European unity in the immediate post-war years, and the British commitment to the defence of Western Europe, the Six had originally been keen to include her in the ECSC. British governments, however, while regarding unity as wholly admirable for Europeans, preferred to remain aloof. Anything that smacked of federalism was anathema to both British political parties. British trade was much more geared towards the Commonwealth and the Sterling Area than towards Europe, and Eden was as lukewarm about the Messina discussions as he had been about British participation in the European Defence Community. According to Butler, 'Anthony was bored with this. Frankly, he was even more bored than I was' [45 *p. 172*]. There was some disagreement in Cabinet over how Britain should react. While Eden wanted nothing to do with the Messina proposals, Macmillan argued that Britain should be fully involved in the discussions, to try to influence European development. He was no more keen than Eden on joining a community that would create supranational institutions, but believed that Britain could challenge American economic power only as leader of both Europe and the Commonwealth. To the surprise of the British, the Six made rapid progress and the 1957 Treaty of Rome established the Common Market which came into existence on 1 January 1958. This was something of a setback for British policy-makers, who had expected the problems of creating the Common Market to be insuperable. But a rather more immediate and dramatic blow to British prestige occurred in Egypt in 1956.

THE SUEZ CRISIS

Since the British withdrawal from India, the Middle East had assumed a central role in British strategic thinking. 'After 1945 the Butskellism of London's foreign policy lay in the cross-party commitment to the maintenance of the British stake along much of the Mediterranean fringe' [117, 1, no. 4 *p. 39*]. Although the United States and Britain differed about European colonialism in the region, they were agreed that the principal threats to stability in the Middle East were the proximity of the Soviet Union to Western oil supplies and strategic bases, and the continued hostility between the Arab states and Israel. As there had been no peace treaty after the Arab-Israeli War of 1948–49, conflict could break out again at any time. To lessen this risk, Britain, France and the United States had signed, in 1950, the Tripartite Declaration by which they sought to limit the supply of arms to the Middle East and agreed to take action against any state attempting to violate the armistice frontiers. Foreign Office officials in both Britain and America were also working in secret on a plan, codenamed 'Alpha', for a comprehensive Arab-Israeli settlement, by which Israel would be asked to surrender territory in the Negev desert in return for Arab recognition of her right to exist. To counter the threat of Soviet penetration, both Britain and America wanted to construct a Middle Eastern equivalent of NATO, but disagreed about its potential membership. The Americans wanted it to comprise the so-called 'Northern Tier' states of Turkey, Iraq, Iran and Pakistan, and opposed Britain's attempts to include Jordan – suspecting, quite rightly, that the British wished to use the alliance as a means of preserving their influence in the Middle East [118]. Eden resented the 'apparent disinclination by the United States Government to take second place even in an area where primary responsibility was not theirs, [which] resulted in the Americans, at least locally, withholding the wholehearted support which their partner in NATO had the right to expect' [27 *p. 256*]. The British version of the Middle Eastern alliance began to take shape when, in February 1955, Turkey and Iraq signed the Baghdad Pact. Britain joined in April and Pakistan and Iran later in the year. Nasser had made Egypt's hostility to the Pact clear to Eden when the two had met in Cairo in February, but the British continued to try, unsuccessfully, to persuade King Hussein of Jordan to join it [104].

This increased diplomatic activity occurred at a time when the situation in the Middle East was more volatile. In 1955 Israeli reprisals became more severe in response to Egyptian-backed terrorist raids launched against Israel from the Gaza Strip. Israel began secret arms negotiations with the French; Egypt, rebuffed by the United States, turned to the communist bloc for military supplies. In September it became clear that the USSR, using the Czechs as intermediaries, had agreed to supply arms to Egypt. This worried both Britain and America, because a hostile Egypt could undermine Western influence in the Middle East and because Egyptian compliance was essential to the success of Project Alpha. On 16 December Britain and America agreed to lend Egypt the money necessary to finance Nasser's project for a high dam at Aswan. The British Cabinet agreed that the loan 'would be of immense importance in restoring the prestige of the West, and particularly of the older European powers in the Arab world generally. In our dealings with Egypt it could be a trump card' [110 *p. 176*].

Early in 1956 British and American perceptions of Nasser changed and the policy of trying to win him over was abandoned. With neither the Arab states nor Israel prepared to contemplate concessions of the sort needed to make Project Alpha workable, the scheme was buried in March. The Americans began to have doubts about the economic viability of the Aswan High Dam project and it became clear that Congress might well oppose any American loan [115]. The last straw for Dulles was when, in May 1956, Nasser recognised the communist regime in China. Eden, too, had by this time become convinced that Nasser was a threat to British interests in particular and Western influence in general. He was particularly incensed when, in March, the young King Hussein of Jordan dismissed General Glubb as Commander of the Arab Legion. Eden was convinced that the dismissal, like the refusal of Jordan to join the Baghdad Pact, was the work of Nasser's pernicious anti-British influence. It is possible that he concluded that British influence and prestige in the Middle East could survive only if Nasser were overthrown [121].

On 19 July 1956 Dulles informed the Egyptians that the Americans were withdrawing their offer of a loan to help build the Aswan High Dam. The British followed Dulles's lead a few days later. Nasser felt insulted by the withdrawal of the loan offer and clearly had to find some other way of paying for the dam. On 26 July he suddenly announced that the Egyptian government was nationalising the Suez Canal Company. This represented a major blow to British prestige. Nearly a third of the ships using the canal were British, and more than two-thirds of Western Europe's oil supplies passed through it. However, as the British Cabinet was ruefully aware, Nasser's coup scarcely amounted to an illegal action [*Doc. 16*]. Indeed, the canal was due to become Egyptian property in 1968 anyway, and Nasser was careful to offer compensation to the shareholders and to ensure that nationalisation posed no threat to the orderly passage of shipping through the canal. But Nasser's action could not be ignored if British prestige in the Middle East was to be maintained. It amounted, said Eden, to Nasser having 'his thumb on our windpipe' [9 *p. 172*]. Eden was also facing domestic pressure. He had been wounded by *The Daily Telegraph* article [*Doc. 2*] lamenting the absence of 'firm government', and he faced criticism from the Suez Group. Acquiescence in Nasser's coup could end his premiership.

Nasser's action was almost universally condemned in Britain. *The Times*, on 27 July, called it 'offensive' and 'a clear affront and threat to western interests'. In the House of Commons debate on 2 August, Gaitskell described Nasser's action as 'terribly familiar. It is exactly the same we encountered with Mussolini and Hitler in the years before the war' [4, *557 col. 1613*]. Unfortunately for Eden, he was unable to take advantage of this sense of national solidarity because an immediate military response was impossible. The experience at Arnhem in 1944 had taught the British army the dangers of airborne landings unsupported by ground troops and air cover. Eden was advised that an adequate invasion force could not be assembled in less than six weeks. He ordered his Chiefs of Staff to prepare an invasion plan and advised President Eisenhower of this. He was determined to use the crisis to destroy Nasser – which meant that, from the outset, British policy was faced with a potential contradiction. In public, the government claimed to be pursuing the honourable goal of international control over one of the world's most important waterways, with force as a last resort should such control be jeopardised by Nasser's action. In private, ministers accepted that force would have to be used to destroy Nasser, except in the unlikely event of a negotiated settlement sufficiently humiliating to ensure his downfall.

The French, who believed the Algerian revolt would collapse without Nasser's help, were also outraged by Nasser's action, because the Suez Canal Company was partly French-owned and had its headquarters in Paris. The French government had none of Eden's scruples and made it plain that they favoured an immediate and forcible response. They stuck consistently to this line throughout the crisis and displayed a singular lack of patience with diplomatic procedures. Eden, however, was aware of the need for American support, particularly if force was to be used. Eisenhower did not agree with Eden's assessment of the threat to Western interests posed by Nasser and, although he accepted that Nasser's action should not go unchallenged, he was implacably opposed to the use of force [*Doc. 17*]. But Dulles, when he arrived in London on 31 July, remarked that 'a way had to be found to make Nasser disgorge what he was attempting to swallow' [*27 p. 437*]. Eden made the miscalculation of assuming that Dulles, and not Eisenhower, ran American foreign policy, and he concluded from Dulles's remark that the American government would support military action by Britain and France if it proved necessary. Dulles was never as unambiguously clear as Eisenhower because he was pursuing slightly contradictory objectives. He wanted a peaceful settlement but did not wish Nasser to succeed. He hoped to restrain Britain and France, but did not want to provide Nasser and the USSR with a propaganda victory by showing that a rift existed between NATO allies. Also, he believed a negotiated settlement might come more quickly if Nasser feared an attack. All this made Dulles's policy hard to fathom, and his apparent shifts and turns during the crisis exasperated Eden.

On 10 August the Chiefs of Staff presented their invasion plan, codenamed 'Musketeer', to the Cabinet's Egypt Committee. They had abandoned the earlier objective of capturing Port Said and now envisaged an assault on Alexandria designed to overthrow Nasser. The invasion fleet would have to sail from Malta (about 1,000 miles or six days' steaming from Port Said) because Cyprus lacked an adequate deep-water harbour. Within a month, though, worries about the number of civilian casualties that would result from the naval bombardment of Alexandria led to another change.

'Musketeer Revise' was presented on 10 September. This switched the emphasis of the allied attack back to Port Said and the canal.

Eden still needed a pretext for invasion and hoped that diplomacy would provide one. A conference of maritime nations held in London in August proposed giving control of the canal to an international board. Nasser rejected this but, with canal traffic unimpeded, his rejection hardly amounted to a *casus belli*. In September there was another London conference, to discuss Dulles's idea of a Suez Canal Users' Association (SCUA) which would hire pilots and collect tolls, thus depriving Nasser of revenues. The British government went along with the scheme, hoping that if Nasser rejected it the Americans would support their use of force [109]. When Dulles announced in public that the Americans would not use force if the Egyptians rejected SCUA, and would re-route their ships around the Cape if necessary, Eden felt betrayed. His growing sense of exasperation with the Americans, and with Dulles in particular, helps to explain why he felt justified in later defying them [121].

In late September Britain and France referred the crisis to the UN Security Council. By that stage there was little else they could do. Eden was painfully aware that military action was impossible without further Egyptian provocation, and this Nasser had studiously avoided. By the time the Security Council started its deliberations, Britain faced further complications in the Middle East. The Israelis had stepped up their reprisal raids against terrorist bases in Jordan and war looked imminent. Britain's treaty with Jordan meant that she was faced with the prospect of preparing for war against Israel and Egypt simultaneously.

It was the French who enabled the British to escape from this dilemma. On 14 October Albert Gazier, the acting French Foreign Minister, and General Maurice Challe arrived in Britain to try to interest Eden in collusion with the Israelis. Challe's plan was simple: Israel would invade Sinai, and Britain and France would intervene to protect the Suez Canal from the fighting. This had obvious attractions for Eden. It would provide the pretext for military action he had fruitlessly sought since July. It could be presented to the world as a police action which might overcome America's scruples about the use of force. With the Israelis fighting Egypt they were unlikely to threaten Jordan, and the results of the war might be sufficiently serious to topple Nasser. Furthermore, Eden, who had just made a belligerent speech on the crisis to the Tory Party Conference, would be spared the criticism of his restless right-wingers anxious for action against Egypt. Possibly this domestic threat was Eden's principal consideration at the time [87; 129].

Meanwhile, at the UN, Lloyd had made some progress and later reported to Cabinet on 'the possibility that we might be able to reach, by negotiation with the Egyptians, a settlement which would give us the substance of our demand for effective international supervision of the Canal' [87 *p. 143*]. There is some doubt as to how close the two sides really were to a negotiated settlement in the UN. The evidence suggests that Lloyd was negotiating in good faith. Eden too, until the Chequers meeting with Gazier and Challe, seems to have been resigned to some sort of negotiated deal. On the other hand, the Egyptians had every reason to spin out the UN negotiations for as long as possible, since they believed that unilateral military action was unlikely while the issue was still being discussed. They also knew that they could rely on the USSR in the Security Council. The collusion plan, however, meant that the British and French governments were no longer interested in a negotiated settlement.

The details of this plan were settled at a series of clandestine meetings outside Paris between French, British and Israeli officials, and the secret Sèvres Protocol [*Doc. 18*] was signed on 24 October. Eden gained Cabinet backing for allied intervention to protect the canal should Israel invade Egypt, but it is not clear how many ministers knew the full details of the collusion plan. In the evening of 29 October the Israelis launched their offensive into Sinai. On 30 October the British and French governments went through the charade of consulting before issuing their pre-arranged ultimatum. Since the Israeli forces had not reached the canal at the time the ultimatum was issued, they were, in effect, being invited to advance while the Egyptians were instructed to withdraw from their own territory. More serious for Eden was the reaction of the Americans. Their Security Council resolution, demanding an Israeli withdrawal and calling on all UN members to refrain from the use of force, was vetoed by Britain and France. This so angered the Americans that they made common cause with the USSR to bring the crisis before the General Assembly. British bombing of Egyptian airfields was carried out during the night of 31 October/1 November. Nasser's response was to order ships filled with concrete to be sunk in the canal. A British bomber conveniently sank one of them for him, and in all nearly 50 ships were sunk in the next 48 hours. On 3 November Nasserite sympathisers blew up an Iraqi oil pumping station. British action had thus succeeded in preventing what the whole operation had been designed to secure: unhindered passage through the canal and the security of Western oil supplies.

On 1 November the Defence Minister, Antony Head, told the Commons about the bombing raids. Gaitskell asked whether a declaration of war had been made and, when Eden refused to answer, passions became so roused that the Speaker was forced to suspend the sitting for half an hour. On the same day, Dulles, speaking in the UN General Assembly, demanded an immediate cease-fire. His resolution was accepted by 65 votes to five early the following morning. Faced with such international criticism, the British government was obliged to agree to a Canadian proposal for the creation of a UN force to take over the role of protecting the canal. This was accepted by the General Assembly by 57 votes to one during the night of 3/4 November. In response to the demand for a cease-fire from the UN General Assembly, Eden announced to the Commons on 3 November that 'police action must be carried through urgently to stop the hostilities which are now threatening the Suez Canal' and that such action would continue 'until the United Nations force is constituted' and until such a force was accepted by both Israel and Egypt [4, 558, *col. 1857–58*]. Thus, the British government, having just been condemned by the UN, was claiming to act on its behalf until such time as the UN force was ready to take over. On 4 November, aware of American, Commonwealth and UN hostility to their action, the British learned that the Egyptians had accepted the UN call for a ceasefire. The pretence that the allied invasion was designed to separate the combatants would now have to be dropped and a new fiction devised. Eden suggested that the invasion force should 'be regarded as advanced elements of the international force or trustees on its behalf' to which 'responsibility for policing the Middle East would be handed over . . . as soon as possible' [35 *p. 566*]. As ministers took the decision to press on with the invasion, they could hear angry demonstrators in Whitehall; Eden's policy had polarised opinion in Britain more sharply than at any time since Munich.

On 5 November the allied paratroops gained control of Port Said. On the following day the troops who had sailed from Malta landed and met only light resistance. But the political pressures on the British government were overwhelming. Eisenhower was outraged by allied landings in Egypt in defiance of the UN General Assembly's vote for a cease-fire. When the pound came under pressure, the American government arranged for the International Monetary Fund to refuse a loan unless the British agreed to an immediate cease-fire. There is some debate as to whether or not Eden was influenced by the message he received from Bulganin on 5 November promising that the USSR would 'crush the aggressors by the use of force' [109 *p. 457*], but a message from Pierson Dixon at the UN that 'we are inevitably being placed in the same low category as the Russians in the bombing of Budapest' [87 *p. 80*] probably did hasten his decision. At 6pm Eden announced to the House of Commons that a cease-fire would come into force at midnight London time. Allied forces had gained control of about one-third of the canal.

Eisenhower, newly re-elected, now proceeded to extract the maximum political advantage from the British climb-down. Eden hoped that, with allied troops in control of at least part of the canal, he would be able to negotiate from a position of strength and secure something of his original aim of placing the canal under international control. But Eisenhower refused to see either Eden or the French Prime Minister, Mollett, and insisted that the proposed UN force to replace the allies should have no contingents from any of the major powers. Although he clearly wanted to keep Soviet troops out of the Middle East, he also wanted to exclude Britain and France. More humiliating for Britain was Eisenhower's insistence that no financial assistance for the beleaguered pound, nor any emergency supplies of oil, would be forthcoming until British troops had been withdrawn unconditionally from Egypt. Although the British government endeavoured to haggle over the terms, the Americans were unmoved. On 24 November the UN General Assembly passed a resolution by 63 votes to five censuring Britain and France and demanding the immediate withdrawal of their troops. Macmillan, whose influence as Chancellor was decisive, warned Cabinet in late November that 'the support of the United States Government for the action which we should need to take to support sterling' was essential but could not be obtained 'without an immediate and unconditional undertaking to withdraw the Anglo-French force from Port Said' [35 *p. 584*]. It was left to Selwyn Lloyd to announce Britain's unconditional withdrawal to the House of Commons on 3 December. On 4 December the United Nations Emergency Force (UNEF) took up positions in Sinai and by 22 December all British and French troops had withdrawn from Egypt.

The Suez Crisis divided the nation in 1956 and is still the subject of historical scrutiny and controversy. Much attention has focused on Eden's handling of it. His premiership was destroyed by Suez and he has continued to receive a bad press from historians. Yet it is difficult not to feel a measure of sympathy for him. Nasser's nationalisation of the canal posed him an insoluble dilemma, one that would probably have defeated anyone else in his position. In the context of 1956, some kind of defeat was inevitable. Britain could not accept Egyptian control of the canal without appearing tamely to surrender its great-power pretensions. And Eden, sensitive to the charges that he was weak and had appeased a latter-day Mussolini by signing the Canal Base agreement in 1954, could not make such a surrender without critics on the backbenches and hawks in his Cabinet baying for his resignation. As one sardonic MP put it: 'Eden had to prove that he had a real moustache' [129 *p. 46*]. On the other hand, unlike Hitler in 1936 or even General Galtieri in 1982, Nasser had done nothing illegal, and Britain's use of force to recapture the canal was bound to divide opinion in Britain and incur worldwide disapproval. This explains Eden's desperate search for an adequate pretext. Perhaps the best he could have hoped for was a solution negotiated at the United Nations. It is likely that he was prepared to settle for this [118] until tempted by the French–Israeli collusion plan. But the common ground that Lloyd and the Egyptian Foreign Minister had achieved at the UN did not amount to a settlement, nor is it certain that Eden's domestic critics would have accepted that a negotiated solution was anything other than a defeat.

Eden was also a victim of his past and his prejudices, a set of assumptions about the world which he shared with many in the Conservative Party and in Britain but which were increasingly anachronistic or erroneous. The first was the patronising attitude towards the Egyptians, who could not be allowed to control the canal because they 'had not the technical ability to manage it effectively' [*Doc. 16*]. Hence the British demand for international control, even though there had been no question of this when the Canal Company was in Anglo-French hands. Yet despite these assumptions about Egyptian incompetence (disproved when the European pilots left in September), Eden believed the nationalisation of the canal to be 'the opening gambit in a planned campaign designed by Nasser to expel all Western influence and interest from Arab countries' [87 *p. 121*]. Although Eden's insistence that Nasser was another Mussolini or Hitler was dismissed by Eisenhower as 'making Nasser a much more important figure than he is' [87 *p. 13*], it was hard for Eden and his generation to escape what they believed to be the lessons of appeasement. Similarly, it was understandable that Western leaders, influenced by the prevailing atmosphere of Cold War in Europe, should misjudge the anti-colonial nationalism of men like Nasser. Eden convinced himself that 'the Bear is using Nasser, with or without his knowledge' [87 *p. 117*] and failed to appreciate that countries like Egypt, which had only recently escaped Western imperialism, had no desire to become satellites of the USSR. Eisenhower was more astute in his view that the kind of gun-boat diplomacy which the British contemplated was much more likely to destroy sympathy for the West in the Middle East than Nasser's inflated ambitions.

There is debate about the extent to which Eden was justified in feeling deceived by Dulles. Eden's sympathetic biographer has argued that, while Eisenhower consistently made clear his opposition to the use of force, 'Dulles hovered in the middle, inconsistent throughout, breathing hot and cold bewilderingly' [35 *p. 475*]. Robert Bowie has challenged this, arguing that 'the basic views of Eisenhower and Dulles . . . were clearly congruent' even if, initially, 'there may have been some differences in nuance' [115 *pp. 213–14*]. Dulles was opaque at times, but Eden can be criticised for believing that the Secretary of State and not the President ran American foreign policy and for too readily assuming that the Americans would acquiesce in Britain's use of force.

Eden's most serious failure was the lack of clarity about his ultimate objective. At one of its first meetings, the Egypt Committee (Eden's inner circle of advisers) decided that, 'while our ultimate purpose was to place the Canal under international control, our immediate objective was to bring about the downfall of the present Egyptian Government' [87 *p. 37*]. But these aims were not necessarily compatible, and throughout the crisis Eden had difficulty reconciling them. Shifting the objective of the invasion plan from Port Said to Alexandria and back again reflected this. So did Eden's scrupulous efforts, which impaired the effectiveness of the invasion, to maintain the fiction that the allied intervention was a police action [*Doc. 19*]. Julian Amery's jibe that Eden was 'Baldwin posing as Bismarck' was cruelly accurate.

Eden, of course, was not acting alone, and recent research has suggested that the Chancellor of the Exchequer, Harold Macmillan, played the role of Lady Macbeth during the crisis. He was, initially, one of the leading hawks in Cabinet and did much to reassure Eden that Eisenhower's opposition to the use of force could be discounted. Eden's press secretary recalls Macmillan, after his visit to Washington in September, telling Eden: 'I don't think there is going to be any trouble from Ike – he and I understand each other –

he's not going to make any real trouble if we have to do something drastic' [118 *p. 213*]. As early as 7 August he had recommended cooperation with Israel and was an enthusiast for the collusion plan devised in October. Macmillan must have known the economic risks he was taking in giving whole-hearted support to Eden's belligerent approach, and he does not appear to have made any contingency plans for coping with the run on the pound that ended the operation and turned him, as Denis Healey observed, into 'the leading advocate of unconditional surrender' [31 *p. 170*]. Since Macmillan was the principal political beneficiary of Eden's failure, the suspicion that he aimed to provide Eden with enough rope to hang himself cannot be entirely discounted.

How important was the Suez Crisis? Although it caused Eden's downfall, its impact on British domestic politics was slight. Despite the deep passions aroused in Britain by the affair, public opinion had not divided along party lines [*Doc. 20*] and the limited impact of the crisis on domestic party politics is shown by the general election of 1959 in which the Tories increased their majority. Suez certainly demonstrated that Britain could not act independently as an imperial power in defiance of America. After Suez, both the USSR and the Americans increased their involvement in the Middle East and Africa, although this might have occurred anyway. Suez also contributed, along with perceptions of British economic weakness, to the realisation that Britain's relationship with America would be one of dependence and not partnership. However, Britain remained an imperial power in the Middle East, even though the pro-British regimes in Iraq and Libya were overthrown shortly afterwards. Suez did not influence the Soviets' decision to invade Hungary, although it certainly undermined the ability of Western leaders to condemn the USSR. Whether it accelerated the process of decolonisation in Africa is open to debate [117], but it is probable that it contributed to the British people's acceptance that their days of imperial grandeur were nearly over. Certainly Macmillan, although unrepentant about Suez, undertook a hard-headed appraisal of British foreign and imperial policy during his premiership. If Churchill's convergent three circles exercised a powerful influence on British foreign policy decisions before Suez, after the crisis Macmillan realised that their convergence was largely irrelevant and that Britain's role in each of them would need to be redefined.

MACMILLAN: THE COLD WAR AND THE EEC

When Macmillan became Prime Minister he retained Selwyn Lloyd as Foreign Secretary because he wanted to demonstrate that he was not apologising for Suez and felt that 'one head on a charger should be enough' [33 *p. 7*]. Also, like Eden, he wanted to run foreign policy himself and valued Lloyd because he was loyal and 'had no ideas of his own' [33 *p. 8*]. Macmillan continued to maintain, as in the House of Commons on 16 May 1957, that 'we are a great world Power and we intend to remain so' [4, *570 col. 436*], but he was aware that such pretensions were based more on bluff than on reality. Because he regarded Britain's alliance with America as crucial, he believed his first task was to repair relations with Eisenhower, and he invented a new whimsy for the basis of the special relationship: Britain would play the role of the Greeks in the new Roman Empire of the Americans. In other words, she would provide the sophistication and America the power. This turned out to be no more realistic than Churchill's three circles, but at least it recognised Britain's diminished status.

Macmillan met Eisenhower in Bermuda in March 1957 and was buoyant about their talks, describing the meeting as 'very pleasant, very friendly, very encouraging, but not at all like an experience in the modern world. More like meeting George III at Brighton' [46 *p. 131*]. The Middle East inevitably dominated the talks. In January the Americans had signalled their commitment to resisting the spread of communism in the region by proclaiming the 'Eisenhower Doctrine', and at Bermuda they agreed to join the military planning committee of the Baghdad Pact. Eisenhower promised to supply Britain with Thor missiles, an arrangement which was to prove the start of British reliance on American nuclear technology.

When, in October 1957, the Soviets launched the world's first satellite, there were fears that the USSR had achieved a technological lead over the West and would shortly be able to deliver nuclear weapons from space. Macmillan visited Eisenhower later in the month and thought the effect of this on the Americans was 'something equivalent to Pearl Harbor' [33 *p. 55*]. The Soviets had also made a series of proposals about limiting nuclear tests. This threatened to divide opinion in Britain, where growing public disquiet was to lead to the formation of CND (the Campaign for Nuclear Disarmament) in 1958. Although the issue of nuclear weapons divided the Labour Party, Macmillan was worried about the extent of middle-class sympathy for disarmament and the possible electoral consequences for the Tories.

Macmillan was convinced that, faced with the double threat of Soviet technology and disarmament propaganda, Western unity was essential. He was delighted when, at their meeting in October 1957, Eisenhower agreed to repeal the McMahon Act by which America was forbidden to share its nuclear secrets and proposed that American nuclear missiles should be based in Europe. This was agreed at a NATO summit in December. Macmillan's visits to Eisenhower healed the wounds of Suez, especially as the continued trouble in the Middle East seemed to have vindicated British policy in 1956. Macmillan noted in his diary in December 1957: 'the Americans . . . wish devoutly that they had let us go on and finish Nasser' [33 *p. 59*].

In 1958 revolutionary turmoil threatened both the stability of the Middle East and the survival of the conservative pro-Western regimes. In February, Egypt and Syria, largely on Egyptian terms, proclaimed their union as the United Arab Republic, and in July the monarchy in Iraq was overthrown in a violent coup. These developments alarmed the Americans as much as the British, so when the Maronite Christian President of Lebanon, fearful of Islamic radicalism, asked the Americans for military assistance to shore up his regime, they obliged and dispatched marines. Worried that he was about to suffer the fate of his relatives in Iraq, King Hussein of Jordan requested British military help. Two battalions of paratroopers were sent to Amman from Cyprus (there was a flurry of panic in London when it was discovered that the aircraft had taken off without permission to use Israeli airspace). These interventions proved successful in stabilising Lebanon and Jordan, and the troops were withdrawn in the autumn. Iraq subsequently withdrew from the Baghdad Pact (thereby leaving it with no Arab members) but, with America's accession, it became the Central Treaty Organisation (CENTO) in 1959 – a grand title for an alliance that proved of limited significance.

In 1958 Macmillan found himself having to respond to Khrushchev's mixture of blandishment and bluster. In March the Soviet leader announced a unilateral suspension of nuclear tests. This was awkward for Britain whose nuclear weapons were still being developed. Pressed to respond to the Soviet announcement, Macmillan declared: 'This is as if, in a football match, one side having scored two goals, asked the opposing team not to play any more' [48 *p. 141*]. But Macmillan could not allow the Soviets to seize the moral high ground, so when the Americans agreed to suspend testing, the British government, in August, announced a similar suspension once its current series of tests was complete. In November Khrushchev initiated a new crisis over Berlin when he decided that it was time to end the arrangements that had prevailed since 1945. Arguing that the division of Germany into two separate states had become permanent, Khrushchev declared that the USSR would sign a separate peace treaty with East Germany and hand over Soviet responsibilities in East Berlin to East Germany. He proposed that Berlin should become a demilitarised free city (which would require the removal of Western troops) and threatened to close the routes between West Germany and West Berlin within six months. Since the withdrawal of troops was inconceivable to Western governments, a crisis as serious as the Berlin Blockade of 1948 seemed imminent.

Macmillan decided to try to break the deadlock by personal diplomacy. With one eye on the forthcoming general election, he engineered an invitation to Moscow in February 1959, arousing scepticism and hostility in both Washington and Bonn. Khrushchev's hospitality turned out to be a typically unpredictable mixture of bonhomie and insult, though Macmillan enjoyed himself by shouting 'double gin' at the crowds when he learned that it sounded similar to the Russian for 'good day'. The visit achieved few tangible results, although, like Churchill and Eden before him, Macmillan was seduced by the talk of a forthcoming summit. He was less pleased when, in August, this turned into a surprise invitation from Eisenhower for Khrushchev to visit Washington, but was mollified when the British press gave him somewhat spurious credit for making the invitation possible. It was the firmness of the West's response to Khrushchev's threats, rather than Macmillan's visit, which led to a softening of Soviet attitudes over Berlin. In May the Soviets agreed to a four-power meeting of foreign ministers in Geneva. This carried on until August and, by maintaining the diplomatic momentum towards a summit, allowed Khrushchev's original six-month deadline to pass without incident and tensions to ease.

The summit was fatally undermined before it began. On 1 May 1960 an American U-2 spy plane was shot down over the USSR. Eisenhower tried initially to claim that the plane had merely strayed off course, but a few days later he admitted that it had been spying. Khrushchev arrived in Paris for the summit determined to exploit the incident to the full. Demanding a humiliating apology from Eisenhower, he left when he did not get it. It is probable that the summit would have achieved little anyway. Other Western leaders were sceptical about its value, and Khrushchev, under domestic pressure to give nothing away, may well have used the U-2 incident as a convenient excuse to end it. Macmillan tried to make light of the failure, commenting of the attire of the Soviet delegation that, 'they may know how to make sputniks, but they certainly don't know how to make trousers' [33 *p. 229*]. In reality, as he recorded in his memoirs, he felt 'disappointment amounting almost to despair' [38 *p. 213*] at the collapse of the summit because, as his private secretary later recorded, 'this was the moment he suddenly realised that Britain counted for nothing' [33 *p. 231*].

In July 1960 Macmillan appointed the Earl of Home to replace Selwyn Lloyd as Foreign Secretary, but continued to dominate policy-making himself, especially as Edward Heath, the spokesman in the Commons, seemed, initially at least, out of his depth. Macmillan achieved a minor triumph at the UN in September. When his speech was interrupted by Khrushchev banging his shoe on a desk, Macmillan responded: 'Mr President, perhaps we could have a translation, I could not quite follow' [38 *p. 279*]. In November the Americans narrowly elected John Kennedy as their new president. Somewhat to his surprise, Macmillan rapidly developed a warm personal relationship with a man who was more than 20 years his junior. This, as John Turner has pointed out, was not wholly advantageous. 'The relaxed intimacy which became apparent whenever the two men met may have shielded Macmillan from a full appreciation of the truth about the relative power of the two nations and the importance attached to the United Kingdom by policy-makers in Washington' [48 *p. 157*]. Indeed, during the major international crises of the Kennedy presidency, although Macmillan was consulted, there is little evidence to suggest that he influenced American policy.

This was apparent from the start. The two men first met in March 1961 when Kennedy consulted Macmillan over the developing crisis in Laos, although the President did not act on the advice he received. Macmillan had no warning of the American attempt to overthrow Castro in the disastrous Bay of Pigs operation in April 1961, but was able to provide consolation and counsel in June when Kennedy visited London after his unsuccessful summit with Khrushchev in Vienna. When the Berlin Wall was erected in August 1961, Macmillan's instinct for caution was shared by Kennedy, who knew that there was little he could do apart from making gestures. Kennedy had indicated as much when, a few days before the crisis broke, he told one of his advisers: 'I can get the alliance to move if [Khrushchev] tries to do anything about West Berlin but not if he just does something about East Berlin' [126 *p. 356*]. Building the Berlin Wall was a brutal way of stopping the flood of refugees escaping to the West, but it did nothing to alter the status of West Berlin – it could almost be said to have reinforced it.

In the wake of the Berlin crisis the Soviets decided to resume nuclear testing, and inevitably the Americans responded in kind. Macmillan, anxious for a complete test ban, told the Commons that Britain would not resume testing unless her security demanded it. When he met Kennedy again in Bermuda in December, he was forced to agree to a bargain whereby the Americans could use Christmas Island, a British possession in the Pacific, for atmospheric tests in return for British underground tests in Nevada. In October 1962, during the Cuban Missile Crisis, Macmillan again played the role of sage counsellor to Kennedy but exercised no real influence over American policy.

During 1962 Macmillan thus found himself facing the inexorable logic of British diminished status in the world and of his own policy of tying Britain to America. He had greeted Kennedy's election by preparing a paper called 'The Grand Design' [*Doc. 21*], in which he recognised that 'Britain – with all her experience – has neither the economic nor the military power to take the leading rôle' and called for 'the maximum achievable unity of purpose and direction' among the nations of the free world to resist the threat of communism. This required Britain to seek closer association with Europe, but achieving that was complicated by Macmillan's own emphasis on partnership with America. As he ruefully observed in his diary for June 1962, 'the more [the Americans] tell the Germans, French etc. that they want Britain to be in, the more they incline these countries to keep us out' [39 *p. 335*].

Macmillan had always wanted Britain to be part of Europe, provided that it was on suitable terms, and he had not supported Eden's lofty disdain of European institutions. From April 1957 the British government pursued its Plan G for the creation of a free-trade area in Europe to include the six countries that were busily setting up the EEC and seven others (Britain, Denmark, Norway, Sweden, Austria, Switzerland and Portugal). In contrast to the EEC, Plan G would not cover foodstuffs and would allow individual nations to set their own external tariffs, thus enabling Britain to maintain its Commonwealth trade. Nor did it envisage the creation of any supranational political institutions. Macmillan appointed Reginald Maudling as a 'travelling salesman' [8 *p. 389*] for Plan G, to try to sell the idea to the six countries of the EEC.

His efforts were ended by a French veto in December 1958 and so the European Free Trade Area (EFTA) was created in 1959 as a rather feeble competitor of the EEC. Europe, the contemporary joke put it, was 'at sixes and sevens'.

It was probably after the collapse of the Paris summit in 1960 that Macmillan decided that Britain would have to apply to join the EEC [*Doc. 22*]. The cancellation of the Blue Streak missile had ended Britain's real nuclear independence, and the success of the EEC contrasted with Britain's palpable economic weakness. But it was not until July 1961 that the Cabinet made the decision to apply. Edward Heath was put in charge of Britain's application while Macmillan himself endeavoured to woo de Gaulle, who was expected to be the real obstacle. British membership, claimed the General, would create 'a colossal Atlantic community under American dependence and leadership which would soon swallow up the European Community' [103 *p. 85*]. His principal fear was that Britain, still proud of its Commonwealth links and its special relationship with the USA, would rival France for mastery of Europe. He suspected that the British were not true Europeans and he may have harboured resentment of Britain's role in the Second World War. As Macmillan acutely observed: 'if Hitler had danced in London we'd have had no trouble with de Gaulle' [33 *p. 319*]. It is likely that de Gaulle always intended to block British entry if necessary, but allowed the negotiations to proceed because he expected them to fail. The potential difficulties were considerable. The Commonwealth countries were expected to oppose the loss of their privileged trade with Britain, their case argued in Parliament by a Commonwealth lobby of Conservative MPs who could rely on the support of the Beaverbrook press.

In the event, a Conservative Parliamentary revolt did not materialise and the Commonwealth Prime Ministers offered no serious opposition at their conference in 1962. Heath's patient diplomacy had won over five of the six countries and settled much of the contentious detail [24], but de Gaulle remained intransigent. Macmillan's attempt to implement his Grand Design and marry the American special relationship with Britain's membership of the EEC reached its denouement in December 1962 when Macmillan visited de Gaulle and Kennedy in turn. At Rambouillet, aware that the Americans were about to scrap Skybolt, the missile they had promised in 1960 to sell to Britain, Macmillan told de Gaulle that he wanted the Americans to provide Britain with Polaris instead. De Gaulle resented this. He believed, quite rightly, that an

Anglo-American nuclear deal would exclude France. On Britain's application to the EEC, Macmillan felt the discussions were 'about as bad as they could be' [39 *p. 354*].

At Nassau Macmillan wrung a Polaris deal from the reluctant Kennedy, but both he and the Americans were aware that this made a French veto of Britain's application to the EEC a virtual certainty. De Gaulle duly obliged at a press conference on 14 January 1963. The Nassau deal was the excuse rather than the reason for de Gaulle's veto, but it showed that Macmillan regarded Britain's independent nuclear deterrent and the American alliance as paramount. It is possible that, had Macmillan been less in thrall to the Americans and willing to countenance nuclear cooperation with the French, de Gaulle's reservations about Britain's European credentials might have been overcome at an earlier stage.

The collapse of Britain's European hopes left Macmillan's foreign policy rudderless, but he did achieve a significant international success in 1963. The Test Ban Treaty signed in August by the USA, the USSR and Britain prohibited nuclear tests in the atmosphere, under water or in space. The ban was incomplete – it still allowed underground tests, since agreement could not be reached about monitoring them. Macmillan played a significant part in persuading the reluctant American administration to sign the treaty and demonstrated that, if Britain could no longer claim equal status with the superpowers she still had a role to play as a broker between them.

R.A. Butler was Foreign Secretary during Home's brief premiership. He visited Washington, where he endured a tirade from President Johnson about Britain's sale of Leyland buses to Cuba, and he was the last Western statesman to visit Khrushchev before his fall [21; 34]. Butler's stewardship of the Foreign Office, after the fevered activity of the Eden and Macmillan years, provided little more than a coda to the foreign policy of the Conservative governments.

ASSESSMENT: ADJUSTING TO DIMINISHED STATUS

The decade of the 1950s was one of unprecedented adjustment for the makers of British foreign policy. All previous twentieth-century British governments had faced the problem of matching Britain's vast overseas commitments to her diminishing resources, but never before had those commitments been shed at such a rapid rate. With them went some, but not all, of the politicians' illusions about Britain's international importance. Perhaps the most remarkable feature of this decline was that few in Britain seemed to mind about it. The Suez Crisis aroused heated passions but they were stilled by the speed and unequivocal nature of Britain's defeat. Growing consumer affluence doubtless helped: if Britain lacked the international power of the USA, she could at least enjoy American films, pop music and Coca-Cola. The Cold War, too, played its part, because few in Britain disputed the need to remain closely allied to the USA, even if the price of American friendship was that Britain should play a subordinate role. Once colonial nationalism made the Empire into an embarrassment and gave the USSR further opportunities for mischief-making, there was very little public resentment over its loss. Perhaps the politicians, too, deserve a little credit for their management of foreign policy. Eden may have overplayed his hand during the Suez Crisis, but the crisis had come about partly because he had accepted the need for Britain to reduce her commitments in Egypt. Macmillan, too, recognised Britain's diminished status, as his dogged pursuit of American friendship and the speed of Britain's colonial withdrawal show.

Illusions remained. Inflated views about the importance of the Commonwealth to Britain's status and trade explain the initial lack of interest in the European Economic Community, although an ambivalent attitude towards Europe has been for centuries, and still is, a part of British culture. The determination to remain an independent nuclear power was achieved at great cost, both financial and diplomatic, as Macmillan's painful negotiations with de Gaulle showed. However, when the Tories lost office in 1964, most people in Britain were reconciled to the country's reduced international status. This was no mean achievement, even if the politicians were the last to recognise it.

4 DEFENCE POLICY AND DECOLONISATION

DEFENCE: FROM CHURCHILL TO SUEZ

After the Second World War the British armed forces returned to their traditional roles: the army policed the Empire, the navy guarded the lines of communication, and the Royal Air Force concentrated on the defence of the United Kingdom itself. In 1946 Attlee's government decided to build an independent nuclear deterrent and reintroduced conscription to provide the manpower for the growing problems of colonial policing. The NATO treaty of 1949 required Britain to contribute to the defence of Europe. When the Conservatives took office in 1951 Britain was making a significant, but relatively small, contribution to the Korean War and had 35,000 troops committed to the counter-insurgence struggle in Malaya. The cost of these extensive commitments was the principal factor shaping defence policy in the 1950s, although Britain's changing foreign and imperial role also played a sizable part. To this extent strategy was the product of political policy. But the relationship worked the other way round as well. The demands of military strategy and the ability of the service chiefs to justify themselves ensured that defence spending remained high and had some bearing on colonial policy – as, for example, in the decision to withdraw from Cyprus but stay on in Aden.

One of Churchill's first decisions was to order a review of defence costs. The Global Strategy Paper of 1952 suggested that the centrepiece of British strategy should be the nuclear deterrent, believed to be cheaper than conventional weapons [*Doc. 23*]. The British atomic bomb, successfully tested in October 1952, would be delivered by a fleet of V-bombers already in production. The paper did not recommend many cuts, because it accepted the army and the navy's insistence that there would be plenty of scope for conventional war after the initial nuclear exchanges of any future conflict. As Michael Dockrill has written: 'British strategy during the early 1950s continued to be dogged by conflicting counsels, intense rivalry between the three services and expenditure beyond what the British economy could bear' [93 *p. 51*]. These problems were exacerbated by Britain's commitment to NATO, and Churchill's government had to face a crisis which threatened to destroy the alliance [132].

In September 1950 the Americans had proposed to rearm the newly created state of West Germany, which would strengthen resistance to the USSR in Europe and enable the Europeans to contribute more to their own defence. But the French were alarmed at the prospect of revived German militarism, especially as their own forces were committed in Indo-China. Their response, in October 1950, was to propose the creation of a European Defence Community (EDC), in which German forces would be integrated into a European army. The Labour government, while happy to see the Germans and French cooperating, had been lukewarm about British participation in the EDC. This attitude was endorsed by Eden when he took over as Foreign Secretary. Speaking in Rome on 28 November 1951, Eden declared that 'British units and formations would not participate in a European army, but that there might be some other form of association' [25 *p. 310*]. In May 1952 a treaty was signed, creating the EDC, but there remained doubts about whether the French Parliament would ratify it without a firmer commitment from Britain. Some Frenchmen even questioned the need for German rearmament at all. During 1952 Eden tried to reassure the French by promising 'to maintain armed forces on the continent of Europe for as long as is necessary' [25 *p. 313*], and in December 1953 the new American Secretary of State, Dulles, tried to bludgeon French opinion by threatening an 'agonising reappraisal' [132 *p. 92*] of the American commitment to Europe should the EDC not be ratified by the French.

In August 1954 the French Parliament rejected the EDC and the future of NATO appeared to be in doubt. Eden was worried that the Americans might adopt a 'China First' policy and abandon Europe. In September he proposed a solution by which West Germany and Italy would be invited to join the Brussels Treaty, which Britain had signed in 1948 with France, Belgium, Holland and Luxemburg. This would be called the Western European Union (WEU). West Germany was to be permitted to join NATO provided it renounced the use of nuclear weapons. To assuage French fears, Eden promised that Britain would maintain four divisions and a tactical air force in Europe for as long as the WEU required. This appeared to be a historic moment – the British were making an unprecedented peacetime commitment to maintain troops on the continent. The French ambassador in London is reported to have wept for joy and proclaimed: 'for fifty years – ever since 1905 – French public opinion has waited for this announcement; and at last we have it' [124 *p. 196*]. Churchill was more sceptical and remarked to his doctor: 'What is all the fuss about? No one in their senses thought we could bring our troops home from the Continent. No one imagined that if Russia decided to march to the West we could sit still and do nothing; if there is a war we are bound to fight' [40 *p. 633*]. Although Eden had insisted on a clause by which Britain could withdraw her troops in the event of an overseas emergency or budgetary crisis, his promise was enough to ensure that the French eventually accepted the WEU. West Germany was admitted to full membership of NATO in 1955.

When Eden became Prime Minister, he, like Churchill before him, tried unsuccessfully to find savings in the military budget. Opposition from the three services, pointing to the wide scope of what they were being asked to do, prevented any cuts. Yet the Suez Crisis revealed that, despite the money being lavished on the armed forces, British military strategic planning had its weaknesses. The 1956 White Paper on Defence suggested that the army should be 'primarily organised so that it can bring force to bear quickly in cold or limited war' [97 *p. 30*], but at the beginning of the Suez Crisis Eden was shocked to learn from his Chiefs of Staff that any assault on Egypt would take six weeks to prepare. Britain, it seemed, had the capability only to take part in nuclear war or to fight communist guerrillas in the colonies. The Middle Eastern General Headquarters had been shifted from Suez to Cyprus in 1955, but the island lacked adequate harbour facilities and the Suez invasion fleet eventually sailed from Malta, which was 1,000 miles, or six days steaming, from Port Said.

DEFENCE: FROM SANDYS TO POLARIS

Humiliation at Suez in 1956 strengthened the hands of politicians wanting to cut the defence budget, and in April 1957 Macmillan's Defence Minister, Duncan Sandys, produced a White Paper that, together with other reforms, sought to alter both the structure and the strategy of Britain's defence establishment. Eden had begun organisational reform by increasing the power of the Minister of Defence to coordinate the competing demands of the three services.

Macmillan continued this, although the abolition of the three ministerial posts for the services and their coordination into a centralised defence structure under the Secretary of State for Defence had to wait until April 1964. Sandys's 1957 White Paper [*Doc. 24*] echoed the 1952 review in stressing 'the commitment to nuclear weapons as the most effective deterrent to war' but went on to say that 'on this basis large conventional forces are not required'. Conscription was to be abolished and the number of men in the army almost halved. The British Army of the Rhine (BAOR) was reduced from 77,000 to 64,000, although RAF Transport Command was to be expanded so that forces could be flown rapidly to trouble spots. Emphasis on nuclear weapons allowed Sandys to argue that the number of RAF fighters could be substantially reduced. The navy's battleships were to be scrapped, but Mountbatten, the First Sea Lord, successfully argued for the retention of its aircraft carriers. Home defence was substantially reduced, on the assumption that there would not be much left to defend after a nuclear attack. Britain's hydrogen bomb was successfully tested in May 1957. In the short term, its delivery would be by V-bomber, but plans were laid to develop a ground-to-ground missile – Blue Streak – that would replace these aircraft.

The priority given to nuclear weapons, combined with the cost of producing them, meant that, during Macmillan's premiership, defence policy was subject to a series of difficult negotiations with the Americans. At their meeting in Bermuda in March 1957 Macmillan had persuaded Eisenhower to supply Britain with Thor missiles, intended merely to bridge the gap until Blue Streak was developed. At a further meeting in October 1957 Eisenhower promised to repeal the McMahon Act, by which America was forbidden to share its nuclear secrets. This had the effect of tying Britain ever closer to the United States and annoying the French, who did not benefit from it.

In February 1960 Blue Streak was cancelled. The Treasury had jibbed at its cost since its inception and by early 1960 the Ministry of Defence was warning that Blue Streak was 'vulnerable to pre-emptive attack' by Soviet missiles. It required 15 minutes to get airborne, but Britain's defences could provide only a four-minute warning of a Soviet nuclear attack. In March Macmillan negotiated a deal with the Americans to buy an air-to-ground missile, Skybolt, which would allow the RAF to continue using their V-bombers. In return, the Americans were to be permitted to build a Polaris nuclear submarine base at Holy Loch in Scotland. It was a deal that exposed significant differences between America and Britain over nuclear strategy. The Americans regarded Britain's independent nuclear weapons as militarily insignificant and politically awkward, since any bilateral deal they made with Britain would be resented by the French and Germans. They believed that Britain should possess nuclear weapons only as part of a NATO force and that she should concentrate instead on increasing her conventional forces in Europe. Neither of these ideas was acceptable to Britain, and by July 1960 one of Macmillan's private secretaries was suggesting to him that 'it might be necessary to recognise that our "special relationship" with the United States is not worth much in real terms' [66 p. 292].

The government also faced domestic criticism over the deal. Not only were there were rumours that the Americans were about to scrap Skybolt, but the prospect of American Polaris submarines on the Clyde, making Glasgow a target for Soviet missiles, added to the growing appeal of CND. Macmillan was unable to reassure doubters that the British government would be consulted before Polaris missiles were fired, because the Americans were not prepared to commit themselves on the issue. The government avoided serious embarrassment in Parliament only because the Labour Party was so divided over nuclear strategy.

Kennedy, who became President in January 1961, differed little from Eisenhower in his attitude towards Britain's nuclear weapons. He believed that 'it would be desirable for the British in the long run to phase out of the nuclear deterrent business' partly because 'their activity in this field is a standing goad to the French' [66 p. 298], but also because he was anxious to pursue nuclear disarmament with the Soviets. He wanted greater emphasis on conventional forces and disapproved of Britain's decision to end conscription. The American decision to cancel Skybolt in November 1962 once again raised doubts about Britain's nuclear strategy. American hostility to the British nuclear deterrent had been made public by the Defense Secretary, Robert McNamara, in June 1962, when he described 'independent national nuclear forces within NATO' as 'dangerous, expensive, prone to obsolescence and lacking in credibility as a deterrent' [66 p. 302]. America wanted European nuclear weapons combined in a NATO multilateral force. The British Government, however, believed that the Americans were morally obliged to provide them with a replacement for Skybolt since, as Macmillan told his secretary, 'the agreement about Skybolt and the agreement about Holy Loch were really part of the same arrangement' [66 p. 31].

When Macmillan met Kennedy at Nassau in the Bahamas in December 1962 he wanted the Americans to supply Britain with Polaris to replace Skybolt. After some tough negotiation Kennedy agreed to provide the Polaris missiles needed to carry British warheads, and a formula was devised to reconcile Britain's claims to independence with Kennedy's view that such missiles should be part of a NATO multilateral force. It read: 'except where Her Majesty's Government may decide that supreme national interests are at stake these British forces will be used for the purposes of international defence of the Western Alliance in all circumstances' [66 *p. 316*]. The Nassau deal preserved Britain's membership of the exclusive nuclear great-power club, but since it was so heavily reliant on the Americans, Britain's nuclear deterrent could hardly be called independent.

Buying from America certainly saved Britain the research and development costs of maintaining her own nuclear programme, but because there was scarcely any diminution of Britain's overseas defence responsibilities, the cuts achieved in the defence budget did not match the scale envisaged in 1957. The determination to remain a great power, especially east of Suez, and the demands of colonial policing stretched the manpower of the forces that Sandys had cut. In 1959 the BAOR was reduced to 55,000, but a further reduction proposed in 1960 was abandoned because of protests from Britain's NATO allies. By the early 1960s the government had modified Sandys's emphasis on nuclear weapons, and the 1962 Defence White Paper argued for a balance to be maintained between conventional and nuclear forces.

Defence policy was closely related to colonial policy. The Suez Crisis had demonstrated the inadequacy of Cyprus as a naval base to replace Egypt, and this contributed to Macmillan's decision to grant independence to the island in 1960. The crises in Jordan in 1958 and Kuwait in 1961 seemed to demonstrate that Britain still had a significant role to play in the Middle East, which is why the British retained air and army bases in Cyprus after independence. Until it achieved independence in 1960, Kenya was seen as a possible Middle Eastern base and £3.5m was spent improving facilities there. Aden was then developed as Britain's principal base in the region, although this, too, rapidly became a colonial headache, as it needed to be secured against nationalist insurgents.

When the Conservatives left office in 1964 Britain's defence policy was still based on the assumption that she was a world power.

Defence agreements with allies and former colonies guaranteed a continued 'east of Suez' role for conventional British forces where over 100,000 service personnel remained. NATO commitments and the nuclear deterrent ensured that defence costs continued to increase despite the efforts of successive governments to reduce them. Savings were made, however: between 1951 and 1964 defence spending was reduced from 7.9 per cent of GNP to 5.9 per cent and manpower in the services dropped from 827,000 to 423,000 [93]. Decolonisation reduced, but did not eliminate, Britain's overseas responsibilities. There had been no fundamental change in the aim of British defence policy, which was to maintain a world role as cheaply as possible. This was a problem that would confront the succeeding Labour government even more starkly than it had the Tories.

DECOLONISATION: POLICY AND PERSPECTIVES

The bulk of the British Empire was dissolved in two short periods. The first was 1947–48, when the Labour government granted independence to India, Pakistan, Ceylon and Burma and ended Britain's mandate in Palestine. The second occurred between 1957 and 1964, when Malaya, the West Indies and Britain's African and Mediterranean possessions achieved their independence. There are three principal reasons for this rapid collapse. First, Britain's declining economic power made it increasingly difficult for her to maintain her empire. Secondly, all European empires found themselves challenged by the emergence of nationalist movements within their colonies. Finally, the international climate of the post-war world was hostile to the existence of European colonial empires. The relative importance of these factors differed over time and from colony to colony. British decolonisation, like the Empire itself, lacks a coherent pattern of easy explanation and is a matter of controversy among historians [90; 91].

The relationship between Britain's economic decline and the loss of her empire is neither straightforward nor linear. Although it is true that Britain increasingly found the expense of maintaining the Empire outweighed the benefits, few of Britain's colonies achieved independence simply for that reason. Indeed, Britain's post-war colonial history suggests that the aim of governments in London, both Labour and Conservative, was to strengthen the economic ties between Britain and her colonies rather than loosen them [*Doc. 25*]. Sometimes, as in the case of Malaya, this involved granting independence in the hope that the newly independent nation would remain part of Britain's informal economic empire while freeing Britain from the burdensome cost of administration and defence. In other colonies, such as Kenya, the attempt to exploit the economy more directly to Britain's advantage created political problems which hastened the end of imperial rule.

The unquestioned assumption that underpinned imperial policy after 1945 was that Britain was, and should remain, a great power. In economic terms, this required Britain to maintain the Sterling Area, a currency and trading bloc that, in 1950, covered about a quarter of the world's trade. The colonies, the dominions (with the exception of Canada) and even, after the war, some European countries, used London as the banking centre for their international earnings and allowed the British government to regulate their dollar purchases. The Sterling Area had helped Britain win the war because goods imported from within the area did not have to be paid for in dollars; instead Britain accumulated debts, known as Sterling Balances, which had the effect of tying the creditor country more closely to Britain. The Sterling Area also helped Britain through its painful period of post-war economic recovery. The dollars earned by the export of Malayan rubber and tin, together with the minerals and foodstuffs of Britain's African colonies, contributed enormously to the dollar pool banked and managed in London. Furthermore, Britain was able to use the Sterling Area as a market for her exports. The countries of the Sterling Area acquiesced in this system because most of them continued to rely on Britain not only as the principal market for their exports but also as their main source of development capital. In 1947, following a run on the pound known as the Convertibility Crisis, the members of the Sterling Area even agreed to restrictive measures that tied them more closely still to a common trade policy determined by Britain.

To maintain this position and ensure that the British Empire and Commonwealth became an economic force in the world to challenge the Americans, Britain encouraged the more extensive development of her colonial economies. Chancellor of the Exchequer Stafford Cripps made this plain in 1947: 'The whole future of the sterling group and its ability to survive depends ... upon a quick and extensive development of our African resources' [2 *p. 113*]. Such development would have the double benefit of increasing the colonies' dollar earnings and providing Britain with guaranteed sources of raw materials which did not have to be paid for in dollars. Unfortunately for Britain, this policy caused social and political changes within colonial societies and contributed to the growth of colonial nationalism. Furthermore, in the 1950s the solidarity of the Sterling Area came under strain: as world economic prospects improved, Commonwealth countries began to diversify their trade and to find alternative markets. Britain herself was unable to continue to provide the investment capital they needed, and as her export performance declined so the attractiveness and value of the pound as a medium of foreign exchange deteriorated. Decolonisation was seen by British policy-makers as a way of arresting the worst effects of these problems. In the words of John Darwin,

> post-war economic vulnerability had driven the British towards a 'forward policy' of colonial development and had sharply raised the value of some of their dependencies: forging new and closer economic links which London was anxious to preserve intact after the formal transfer of power. What impelled the British towards the promise of self-government was not anticipation of imminent economic decline, but the pragmatic discovery that a steady devolution of power was the price of stability and cooperation in a developing colonial economy. [90 *p. 243*]

As a challenge to British rule, colonial nationalism was nothing new, but it was greatly stimulated by the Second World War. In the Far East, Britain's imperial prestige had been severely damaged by the fall of Singapore in 1942, and the nationalist guerrilla movements which sprang up to oppose the Japanese could not easily be eradicated after the war. In Africa, wartime colonial rule became more oppressive as the British sought to exploit more effectively the economic resources of their empire. Most colonial administrations, in an effort to appease potential opponents of these policies and to demonstrate to the world that British colonial rule was benign, extended the participation of colonists in their own government. Many aspiring black African politicians spent time during the war in the United States where they were influenced by, and shared the aspirations of, black Americans. They also drew inspiration from the success of Indian nationalism in 1947.

Britain's response to colonial nationalism in its post-war empire was not uniform. In Kenya and Cyprus nationalist guerrilla movements were vigorously and violently opposed, but in other territories, such as the Gold Coast, nationalist politicians were appeased. To some extent the British response to colonial nationalism depended on the perceived economic and strategic value of the colony to Britain, and on a calculation in London as to whether British interests would best be served by repression or capitulation. In many African colonies the British fostered colonial nationalism rather than suppressed it. This was because they wished, first, to try to blend the tribal rivalries and regional diversity of the colonies into viable economic and political units and, secondly, to construct colonial constitutions and hand over power to political parties that would, after independence, ensure the survival of as much British influence as possible. For Britain it was essential to proceed gradually, because premature independence would, as a Foreign Office paper of 1959 stated, 'run the risk of leaving large areas . . . ripe for Communist exploitation' [116 *p. 487*]. But Britain's leisurely timetables were rudely overthrown because, once unleashed, vociferous colonial nationalism proved hard to contain – especially after 1956, when an international situation inimical to European imperialism combined with economic weakness in Britain to hasten imperial retreat.

The Second World War not only altered Britain's relationship with her colonial empire; it also created a bi-polar world dominated by the Cold War struggle between the USA and the USSR. The shrinking power and importance of Europe, and the ideological opposition to colonialism of both superpowers, called into question the survival of European empires. The Chinese revolution of 1949 was an additional stimulus to anti-colonial movements in the Far East. But the Cold War also provided a lifeline for European colonial empires. The Americans increasingly came to regard European rule as preferable to communism, and even attempted in the 1950s to shore up French rule in Indo-China. The threat of communism also enabled the British, most notably in Malaya, to renew their alliance with the indigenous conservative groups in colonial society and to justify continuance of their rule. With America committed to the defence of Europe by the NATO treaty of 1949, the British felt able to disperse their forces around the globe to protect their imperial commitments.

In the late 1950s the international climate turned decisively against European colonialism. To some extent this was a direct result of the Suez Crisis. Nasser had demonstrated to fellow members of the newly formed non-aligned movement that former colonial states could manoeuvre to advantage between the USA and the USSR; imperial tutelege was not the only alternative to communism. The Suez Crisis also precipitated the fall of the Fourth

Republic in France and de Gaulle's decision to grant independence to France's troublesome African colonies. This, followed by Belgian withdrawal from the Congo in 1960, made the British Empire seem anachronistic. The USSR was not slow to denounce it as such in the United Nations, which, with increased Third-World membership, became a forum for anti-colonial rhetoric and for competition between the United States and the Soviet Union for influence among the non-aligned countries.

This hostile international context combined with the force of colonial nationalism and Britain's economic weakness to drive Britain hastily out of Africa between 1957 and 1964. To Harold Macmillan, Prime Minister for most of this period, Britain's imperial retreat appeared to be a victory, the fulfilment of a benign and paternalistic purpose. The British people, he wrote in his memoirs, 'had not lost the will or even the power to rule. But they did not conceive of themselves as having the right to govern in perpetuity. It was rather their duty to spread to other nations those advantages which through the long course of centuries they had won for themselves' [38 *p. 116–17*]. Historians are sceptical about this claim. The evidence suggests that the British established, not stable new nations enjoying the fruits of British sagacity and experience, but political systems and constitutional arrangements that were the products of compromise and haste. It is also clear that the decision about when and how to go differed from colony to colony. Each imperial withdrawal has its own distinctive history.

MALAYA

When it took office in 1951 the Conservative government inherited a major colonial crisis in Malaya. The history of the Malayan Emergency demonstrates Britain's willingness to continue exercising imperial responsibilities and her ability to do so when assisted by favourable local circumstances [*Doc. 26*]. The dollar earnings of Malayan rubber and tin and the strategic importance of Singapore made the Malayan peninsula vital to Britain, although the cost of suppressing the communist insurgents, estimated by the incoming Tories at £56m per annum, was causing concern in London. The aim of British policy was to create a Dominion of South-East Asia which, through its membership of the Sterling Area and defence agreements with Britain, would provide Britain with all the advantages of empire without the burdens and costs of government. Progress towards Malayan self-government would also outflank international criticism and undercut the appeal of communism, now dangerously close in China. As the Labour Colonial Secretary explained to the Cabinet in 1950, constitutional progress was necessary 'to demonstrate to the workers in Malaya that a non-Communist regime offered them greater opportunities for economic and social betterment than any Communist regime' [128 p. 72].

The problem was uniting the Malay, Chinese and Indian communities to form a single, stable nation. In 1941 the population of Malaya (including the predominantly Chinese-populated city of Singapore) was 43 per cent Chinese, 41 per cent Malay and 14 per cent Indian. In 1946 the British introduced a new constitution which gave citizenship to all three communities. The Malays protested vigorously and formed a nationalist party, the United Malays National Organisation (UMNO), to oppose it. The British backed down because they realised they could not afford to alienate the Malays if the Malayan Communist Party (MCP), already active among the Malayan Chinese community, was to be defeated. In February 1948 the Federation of Malaya was created. This restored the domination of the Malays by withdrawing citizenship from all but a few Chinese and Indians. In June 1948, in response to terrorism by the MCP, a state of emergency was declared. The communists proved difficult to defeat. They operated from the jungles and gained food and information from the Chinese squatter villages which had grown up on the jungle fringes.

When the Conservatives took over in Britain, morale over Malaya was at a low ebb. On 5 October the communists had assassinated the British High Commissioner, Sir Henry Gurney, and in 1951 succeeded in killing their highest number of security forces and civilians. Churchill dispatched his new Colonial Secretary, Oliver Lyttelton, to Malaya. On arrival, Lyttelton announced that 'to restore law and order is the first thing' [128 p. 83] and repeated Britain's pledge to grant Malaya self-government within the Commonwealth. The new High Commissioner, who was also to be Director of Operations, was General Sir Gerald Templer. He gave new energy to the counter-insurgency policy and improved morale. He also built on the success of his predecessor as Director of Operations, General Sir Harold Briggs, who had initiated a policy of evacuating the Chinese squatters from the jungle fringes to new villages, thereby depriving the insurgents of both their rice and their intelligence information.

Politically, the British backed Dato Onn bin Ja'afar, leader of

UMNO, because he wanted it to become a multi-racial party. They regarded his policy as the best hope of bridging the gulf between the Malays and the Chinese, without which a stable, post-colonial government seemed impossible. However, in September 1951 Dato Onn abandoned UMNO when it rejected his attempt to open it to non-Malays, and founded a new party called the Independence of Malaya Party (IMP). The new leader of UMNO was Tunku Abdul Rahman who, somewhat to the surprise of the British, forged an alliance with the Malayan Chinese Association to defeat Dato Onn's IMP in local elections. In 1955, now joined by the Malayan Indian Congress, the Alliance won all but one of the elected seats on the Legislative Council. Tunku Abdul Rahman became Chief Minister and head of the first representative government of Malaya. Although the Alliance was not the genuine multi-racialism the British had hoped for, their response to its victory was to bring forward the date for Malayan independence to August 1957. Establishing a government, dominated by conservative Malays, which was willing to remain within the Sterling Area, was too good an opportunity to miss, especially at a time when, elsewhere in South-East Asia, communism appeared to be on the march.

WEST AND EAST AFRICA

British policy in West Africa in the 1950s had the same aims as in Malaya. Anxious to develop her world role independent of the USA, Britain sought to build her colonies into economic partners who would remain loyal members of the Sterling Area. Such development would require limited constitutional reform in each colony to ensure that, once dominion status was granted, post-colonial politics would be dominated by pliant conservatives loyal to the British connection. The British found, however, that their slow, methodical timetable was overwhelmed by the speed of events, and independence came more quickly than anticipated in the Gold Coast (now Ghana) and Nigeria.

In the Gold Coast, British policy during the Second World War and the growing importance of the cocoa crop had opened a rift between the conservative, inland region, still dominated by traditional chieftains, and the commercially farmed southern region served by rapidly developing coastal towns. After riots in 1948 in Accra, the colonial government introduced a new constitution which granted universal suffrage and transferred responsibility for internal government to an elected assembly. The aim was to appease the

United Gold Coast Convention (UGCC), which had been formed in 1947 by a wealthy lawyer to campaign against the power exercised by the traditional chieftains. The UGCC were the kind of conservative nationalists to whom the British wished to transfer power. The beneficiaries, however, of the constitutional changes were the Convention People's Party (CPP) led by Kwame Nkrumah, whose base of popular support was far wider than that of the UGCC. Nkrumah had been demanding immediate self-government, and in 1950 had begun a campaign of strikes and the boycott of British goods, which resulted in his imprisonment. The CPP won the elections in February 1951. Nkrumah himself was elected in Accra despite being in gaol. Governor Sir Charles Arden-Clarke, who a few months earlier had described Nkrumah as a 'local Hitler' [111 *p. 447*], was obliged to release him and appoint him leader of government business – in effect, Prime Minister.

Arden-Clarke and Nkrumah then became allies in pushing forward the process of self-government. Arden-Clarke justified his policy by arguing: 'You cannot slow down a flood – the best you can hope to do is to keep the torrent within its proper channel' [111 *p. 455*]. For the British, Nkrumah had become the 'proper channel' because he aimed for independence within the Commonwealth and the Sterling Area. Both men hoped that a second general election in 1954 would be the prelude to independence. Although the CPP won the election, it was clear that the central (Ashanti) and the Northern Regions were anxious about domination by the southern and coastal regions which formed the bulk of the CPP's constituency. The extent of this potential opposition made the British require a third election before granting independence. Nkrumah was able to widen the basis of support for the CPP in Ashanti and the Northern Regions by playing on the traditional tribal rivalries, and duly won a majority in the election of July 1956. The British also insisted that independent Ghana should have a federal constitution; a concession that Nkrumah was willing to make because, as he admitted to his secretary, 'I can drive a coach and horses through this constitution and after independence I certainly will' [111 *p. 461*].

To the British Colonial Office the independence achieved by Ghana on 6 March 1957 was almost a model of ordered withdrawal. It had been achieved with the minimum of violent confrontation, and power had been handed to a regime that, by remaining within the Sterling Area, appeared to guarantee the future of Britain's economic interests. Ghana's subsequent history was to belie this optimism.

In nearby Nigeria the problem of regional differences was even more marked than in Ghana. One Nigerian chief, in a conscious echo of Metternich's famous description of early nineteenth-century Italy, said: 'Nigeria is not a nation. It is a mere geographical expression' [88 *p. 37*]. The north of the colony was Muslim, traditional and rural; the south Christian, more commercial and westernised. The southern region was divided between two dominant tribes: the Ibo in the east and the Yoruba in the west. As in the Gold Coast, the British introduced a series of constitutions in an effort both to keep the colony together and to ensure the transfer of power into safe hands. The 1954 constitution was federal, and in the 1959 elections the Northern People's Congress emerged as the largest party, but without an overall majority. Support in the south was divided between the Ibo-dominated National Council for Nigeria and the Cameroons (NCNC) and the Yoruba-dominated Action Group. Fear of the Action Group forced the Northern People's Congress into coalition with the NCNC. It was this coalition that was in power when Nigeria achieved independence in October 1960. Britain's other West African states, Sierra Leone and The Gambia, despite doubts about their economic and political viability, achieved independence in 1961 and 1965 respectively.

Similar nation-building problems were evident in Britain's possessions in east and central-southern Africa where, in some colonies, there was the complication of extensive white and Asian settlement. The British settlers who started arriving in Kenya towards the end of the nineteenth century began the successful plantation of crops such as coffee and tea. This made Kenya much richer than Britain's other East African colonies. Between the wars the whites established exclusive control over a block of land in the centre of the colony known as the White Highlands. Their numbers were swollen after the Second World War in what has become known as the 'second colonial occupation', when the British government decided on a policy of extensive colonial economic development. All of this gave the white settlers political power disproportionate to their numbers. The Asian community, also first established in the 1890s, dominated the commercial life of Kenya while the indigenous black population, divided between three principal tribes – the Kikuyu, Masai and Luo – were mostly peasant farmers. The Kikuyu, in particular, resented their exclusion from the White Highlands, which they regarded as their ancestral land.

The aim of the Kenyan whites was to achieve the kind of self-government exercised by the whites in South Africa and

Southern Rhodesia. This would enable them to secure domination of Kenyan society. British governments were still bound by the White Paper drawn up by the Colonial Secretary in 1923, which stated: 'primarily Kenya is an African territory, and His Majesty's Government think it necessary definitely to record their considered opinion that the interests of the African nations must be paramount, and that if and when those interests and the interests of the immigrant races should conflict, the former should prevail' [88 *pp. 40–1*]. This placed the British in a dilemma: reluctant to hand over power to a white minority, they could not afford to alienate the whites who not only were responsible for most of Kenya's wealth but enjoyed articulate support in Britain. The aim of British policy was to develop multi-racial institutions that would guarantee the rights of all three communities, but as there were few Africans experienced in democratic statecraft or administration, the colonial authorities believed that independence was a long way off.

The post-war policy of developing the Kenyan economy threatened to increase still further the power and influence of the white community and exacerbated the Kikuyu anger at their exclusion from the White Highlands. Their resentment turned ugly in the Mau Mau rebellion of 1952–56. Although hostile to European rule, the Mau Mau terrorists directed their violence more against fellow Kikuyu – those who were regarded as collaborators – than against Europeans. During the troubles 95 whites were killed, but more than 14,000 Kikuyu. The Mau Mau insurgents were vigorously suppressed by the British authorities, and Jomo Kenyatta, the charismatic Kikuyu leader, was gaoled in 1953. But the rebellion did alter the politics of Kenya. The white colonists could not suppress Mau Mau without the help of British troops, which made it clear that the settler goal of an independent state was unrealistic. To reward loyal Kikuyu and prevent the spread of Mau Mau to other tribes, constitutional reforms in 1954 and 1958 increased African representation in the administration. In 1954 the Swynnerton Plan was introduced to develop commercial farming among the Africans. The aim was to undercut the appeal of Mau Mau by increasing the prosperity and stability of African rural life. The British did not envisage immediate independence for Kenya. After their withdrawal from Egypt, Kenya assumed a new importance in British strategic thinking as the key to the defence of both Africa and Britain's Far Eastern interests. A conference of the governors of Britain's East African colonies early in 1959 suggested that Kenya might become independent by 1975.

Following his election victory in October 1959, Macmillan decided to accelerate the pace of change in Africa. As his new Colonial Secretary, Macmillan appointed Iain Macleod, a man committed to black majority rule. Macleod convened a constitutional conference in London in January 1960, attended by African politicians, and he hoped to persuade them to work with, and perhaps join, the New Kenya Group (NKG), a multi-racial party recently formed by a white settler named Michael Blundell. Although Macleod stubbornly refused the black Kenyans' demand for the release of Kenyatta, the conference did devise a constitution which gave Africans a majority in the legislative assembly. The Africans now formed two parties, the Kenya African National Union (KANU), which drew its support from the Kikuyu and Luo, and the Kenya African Democratic Union (KADU), which was supported by the Masai and others fearful of Kikuyu domination. After the election of 1961, KADU, supported by the NKG, took power. To avoid appearing to be tools of the British, they demanded the release of Kenyatta and further reform. Kenyatta was duly released and there was another constitutional conference in London in 1962. In the election of May 1963 Kenyatta and KANU won a large majority, and in December 1963 Kenya became independent.

The main stumbling-block to independence in neighbouring Uganda was a legacy of pre-colonial days. The area which became Uganda had been four separate, antagonistic kingdoms, the most powerful of which was called Buganda. In 1952, in accordance with British colonial policy elsewhere, the newly appointed governor announced: 'the future of Uganda must lie in a unitary form of central Government on parliamentary lines covering the whole country' [88 *p.* 39]. This was anathema to the Kabaka (king) of Buganda, Mutesa II. His opposition provoked the governor into deposing him and having him deported to London in 1953. Disquiet over this in Britain led to the appointment of a commission and a constitutional conference in 1954. This declared that the future of Uganda was to be 'African', and the British authorities, although they released Mutesa in 1955, set about fostering all-Uganda nationalism in a bid to undercut Bugandan separatism. It was not difficult to play on the other tribes' fear of Bugandan domination. The tactic appeared to have failed when, in December 1960, the Bugandan Parliament voted for secession. However, in June 1961 Buganda was offered federal status. In 1962 the Kabaka formed an alliance of convenience with Milton Obote, the leader of the Uganda People's Congress, because both feared the growing popularity of the Democratic Party. On the basis of this uneasy compromise, the British – anxious to avoid policing the different factions – granted Uganda independence in October 1962.

Britain had ruled Tanganyika only since 1919, when she received it as a League of Nations mandate, but this did not stop her planning to incorporate it, with Kenya and Uganda, into an East African Federation. Although this idea was dropped, British policy in the colony followed the familiar pattern of encouraging rapid economic development and promoting multi-racial politics. Both served to aggravate black nationalism. Since the white settler community was smaller than in Kenya, the black Africans feared that multi-racial policies would give the whites greater power than their numbers warranted. In 1954 Julius Nyerere formed the Tanganyika African National Union (TANU) to oppose British multi-racial policies, and in 1958 it won the elections to the new legislative council. With Macleod in the Colonial Office, Tanganyika's progress to independence in 1961 proceeded rapidly. In 1964 Tanganyika united with Zanzibar, which had achieved independence in 1963, to form Tanzania.

THE CENTRAL AFRICAN FEDERATION

Britain's most intractable African problem was in her central-southern colonies. In 1953 Northern and Southern Rhodesia and Nyasaland had come together to create the Central African Federation, but the character of each was very different. The territory north and south of the Zambesi river, which became Northern and Southern Rhodesia, was colonised in the late 1880s by Cecil Rhodes's British South African Company. It continued to be administered by the Company until the early 1920s, when Northern Rhodesia became a crown colony and Southern Rhodesia, in deference to the sizable and articulate white settler community, a self-governing colony. Under this unique constitutional status Southern Rhodesia was not a dominion but was treated as such, although the British government retained some rights over her legislation. Northern Rhodesia had a much smaller white community but was rich in copper. Nyasaland, with a mainly agricultural economy, was an impoverished drain on the British exchequer and contained few whites.

Each of the parties to the Federation of 1953 embraced it for different reasons. The British government believed that the white Afrikaner regime in South Africa harboured expansionist aims and that federation would enable the Central African territories to resist. It argued that economically the territories were already interdependent and, as a Cabinet paper of November 1951 recommended, 'development ought to proceed on a Central African basis so that the resources of the whole region may best be devoted to economic advancement' [*Doc. 27*]. Nyasaland could be freed of its dependence on the British Treasury and greater economic prosperity would overcome black African opposition to the scheme. The accretion of large black populations would act as a counter-weight to white nationalism, so that the Federation could be developed as truly multi-racial.

The white communities either side of the Zambesi had long wanted to amalgamate. Those in Northern Rhodesia aspired to the virtually independent status enjoyed by Southern Rhodesia, while the copper wealth of the north was an obvious attraction to those in the south. Both white communities were worried by the growth of white Afrikaner migration into Rhodesian territory and regarded amalgamation as the only way to retain their separate identity. Although federation was not amalgamation, it was clear that the new state would be dominated by the whites. This is also why black African opinion rejected and opposed it, believing that the Federation was the first step towards their abandonment by Britain into a state, not unlike South Africa, in which their subjection to white rule would be permanent.

John Darwin has described the Central African Federation as 'an exotic constitutional beast' [92 *p. 200*]. The federal government, elected on a mostly white franchise in each territory, was responsible for finance, trade, transport and defence. Its relations with London were handled by the Commonwealth Office. Britain created an African Affairs Board with the power to refer any discriminatory federal legislation to London, and insisted on a constitutional review of the Federation within ten years. Each territory had its own government which controlled education, welfare and the police. In Southern Rhodesia the government was responsible to a legislature elected entirely by whites; the other two territories were ruled by an executive governor, appointed by, and responsible to, the Colonial Office in London. These cumbersome arrangements help to explain why the Federation became a divisive issue in British domestic politics between 1959 and 1963.

For the first three years of its life the Federation appeared to justify the British government's faith in it. Rhodesian copper was earning high prices on international markets, although the

Federation's tax policies ensured that most of the benefit went to Southern Rhodesia. Increased wages muted, but did not dissolve, black opposition. In 1957 the Federal Parliament passed a Constitutional Amendment Act designed to entrench white domination more firmly. The African Affairs Board disapproved but was overruled by the British Parliament. This stimulated black opposition to the Federation, because it seemed clear that the white ambition of dominion status would be granted by the forthcoming constitutional review (now expected in 1960) and that the British government paid only lip-service to the interests of black Africans. In 1958 Dr Hastings Banda returned to lead the Nyasaland Congress Party (NCP), and in Northern Rhodesia, Kenneth Kaunda, already active in fomenting strikes and boycotts, founded the Zambia African National Congress (ZANC). They were encouraged by support from Nkrumah in Ghana and by the knowledge that the Labour Party in Britain was hostile to the Federation.

In March 1959 the governor of Nyasaland declared a state of emergency following some riots. Banda and 120 members of his party were arrested. The governor went further and claimed that Banda was planning a massacre of Europeans, and this view was endorsed in the House of Commons by the Colonial Secretary, Alan Lennox-Boyd. Policing the emergency resulted in the death of 51 Africans and the wounding of 79 more. In response, the British government appointed a commission of enquiry under Mr Justice Devlin, which reported in July and concluded that there was no evidence that Banda and the NCP had plotted 'massacre and assassination'. The report went on to describe Nyasaland as 'no doubt temporarily – a police state' [66 p. 235]. The publication of the report coincided with the news that Kenyan police had beaten to death 11 Mau Mau detainees at the Hola detention camp and brought colonial issues to the forefront of British domestic politics. Macmillan repudiated the Devlin Report and the Cabinet gave its backing to the beleaguered Colonial Secretary, but, according to Alistair Horne, 'Devlin seems to have sowed the first strong seeds of doubt in Macmillan's mind as to whether the Federation had any future at all' [33 p. 182].

The problems of the Federation exposed a number of difficulties for the Macmillan government. The white settlers of Kenya and the Federation were strongly supported by an articulate lobby in the Tory Party, while the Labour Party was united in condemning the Federation's policies towards its black majority and was highly critical of heavy-handed colonial policing. The independence of

Ghana had increased the expectations of black African politicians, and Macmillan feared that the growing international hostility to European colonial empires had become a factor – to the disadvantage of the West – in the Cold War against communism. He quailed at the thought of the lengthy counter-insurgency campaigns that would be necessary to keep black nationalism in check, and he knew that the manpower for them would be in short supply because conscription had been abolished by the 1957 Defence Review. In June 1959 the Foreign Office advised that 'the Federation may simply break up under the mounting pressure of internal conflict' [116 *p. 489*], but Macmillan was reluctant to arrange its immediate demise. He wanted it to survive, but in a genuinely multi-racial form, and feared that, if it collapsed, any ensuing chaos could be exploited by the USSR and that Southern Rhodesia would either join South Africa or embarrass Britain by demanding independence. He was also aware of the need to appease the imperialist lobby within his own party, who felt that promoting black majority rule was an abandonment of Britain's white African 'kith and kin'. The granting of independence to the former Belgian Congo in June 1960 exacerbated the problems. Its immediate descent into civil war confirmed white African fears of the effects of black majority rule, but also made it more difficult for Britain to cling on to empire as European rule in Africa receded.

The future of the Federation became a bitterly contentious issue in British domestic politics for the next three years. Macmillan took a close personal interest and appointed himself chairman of the Cabinet Africa Committee in October 1959, but he offered ambiguous signals about the Federation's future. In March 1959 the British government announced the establishment of the Monckton Commission to advise on the Federation's future and gather evidence for the forthcoming constitutional review. Macmillan told Sir Roy Welensky, the belligerent white Prime Minister of the Federation, that the Commission would not examine the issue of secession, but in private said the opposite to a former Labour minister who agreed to join the Commission. In January 1960, when in Ghana at the start of his African tour, Macmillan outraged Welensky by announcing that Northern Rhodesia and Nyasaland 'will be given an opportunity to decide on whether the Federation is beneficial to them' [33 *p. 191*], but endeavoured to mollify him when they met by reiterating his faith in the future of the Federation. In Nyasaland, Macmillan found, as he recalled in his memoirs, that 'the cause of the Federation was almost desperate because of the strength of African opinion against it' [38 *p. 148*]. By early February Macmillan was in Cape Town, where he reminded the South African Parliament that 'the wind of change is blowing through this continent, and, whether we like it or not, this growth of national consciousness is a political fact. We must all accept it as a fact, and our national policies must take account of it' [*Doc. 28*].

This speech, and the choice of Macleod as Colonial Secretary in October 1959, clearly indicated, as Macleod himself later wrote, 'a deliberate speeding-up of the movement towards independence' [7 *p. 570*]. But this only brought the political problems into sharper focus. Welensky loathed Macleod and found an ally in the Earl of Home, the Commonwealth Secretary. Macleod and Home clashed over whether or not Banda should be released to give evidence to the Monckton Commission and over the pace of change. Home recommended in a letter to Macmillan of June 1960 'a programme of advance culminating in independence for Nyasaland and Northern Rhodesia in 1970' [66 *p. 252*], whereas Macleod was clearly thinking in terms of months, not years. These issues threatened the unity of the Cabinet, and Macleod's resignation was only averted by Banda's release in April 1960, shortly before the Commission left Africa. Banda himself chose not to give evidence to it, but he did attend Macleod's London conference in June on the constitution of Nyasaland, which extended the electorate to guarantee an African majority in the legislature. This made Nyasaland's secession from the Federation only a matter of time.

Welensky and the government of Southern Rhodesia were less concerned with Nyasaland than with Northern Rhodesia. Consequently, they were outraged by the recommendations of the Monckton Commission, which reported in October 1960 [*Doc. 29*]. Although, like Macmillan, the Commission wanted the Federation to survive as a multi-racial partnership, it suggested that the right to secede should be acknowledged. It recommended parity of black and white representation in the Federal Assembly, changes in the racial laws of Southern Rhodesia, and African majorities in the legislatures of Nyasaland and Northern Rhodesia. To many observers the Monckton Commission signalled the end of the Federation. As a result, the conference to review the federal constitution, which convened in December, was adjourned without achieving anything.

The year 1961 was dominated by further conferences on the constitutions of each of the Rhodesias. Macmillan did not emerge with credit – his policy during this period has been described by his biographer as 'patching and fudging' [33 *p. 391*] – and it is possible that the damage done to his reputation over his handling of the issue contributed to his fall from power in 1963. He was trying to achieve two difficult objectives. The first was to prevent the death of the Federation by finding constitutional formulae for each Rhodesian territory that would advance the interests of the black majorities without alarming the whites. He was also trying to hold his government and party together by reining in Macleod's enthusiasm without capitulating to the entrenched imperialism espoused by Lord Salisbury, one of the party's influential grandees.

The conference in Salisbury on constitutional change in Southern Rhodesia agreed a small advance in African representation, but the major battle was fought over the constitution of Northern Rhodesia. There were bitter rows over Macleod's liberal draft, and he was attacked in the House of Lords by Lord Salisbury for being 'too clever by half'. Macmillan and others toned down his draft and in June 1961 devised a formula with which Welensky could agree. It provoked outrage and renewed violence in Northern Rhodesia, where the blacks, led by Kenneth Kaunda, wanted nothing less than majority rule and independence. In December 1961 Macmillan appointed Reginald Maudling to the Colonial Office in place of the troublesome Macleod, but soon found him 'more difficult and intransigent than his predecessor' [33 *p. 408*]. Maudling wanted to abandon the formula devised in June and produced a draft much more favourable to black opinion. Despite the risk of further government disunity, a new franchise for Northern Rhodesia was announced in the House of Commons in February 1962. It differed little from Macleod's proposal of a year before and made African majority rule a certainty. Macmillan had now accepted that the Federation was doomed and lost interest in central Africa. In March he appointed R.A. Butler to head the newly created Central African Office which was to take over the Rhodesian problem from the Colonial Office and the Commonwealth Office and to perform the obsequies of the Federation. In December 1962 Butler announced that Nyasaland would be permitted to secede, and after elections in Northern Rhodesia in October, which produced a black government demanding secession and independence, a similar statement on its future was made in March 1963. The Federation was formally dissolved on 31 December 1963, and in 1964 Nyasaland became independent Malawi and Northern Rhodesia independent Zambia. That left Southern Rhodesia, where the elections held in December 1962 had been won by the newly formed Rhodesia Front, demanding independence on the basis of white minority rule. This was something that no British government could grant without destroying the Commonwealth and facing a storm of protest in the UN. On the other hand, conscious that perhaps as many as 200 Conservative MPs sympathised with the white regime in Southern Rhodesia, Macmillan's government lacked the will to confront it. In November 1965 the white Rhodesia Front government announced its Unilateral Declaration of Independence and made that colony as irksome to Harold Wilson's Labour government as the Federation had been to Macmillan's.

OUTPOSTS AND THE COMMONWEALTH

Cyprus, too, proved troublesome to deal with. A British protectorate since 1878, Cyprus was annexed from Turkey in 1914 and became a crown colony in 1925. Its population was 80 per cent Greek and 20 per cent Turkish. In 1931 the constitution was suspended and authoritarian British rule was imposed after riots inspired by the Greek Cypriot demand for union with Greece (*enosis*). During the Second World War Greek Cypriots fought with the British against the common German enemy and in 1948 Britain offered limited self-rule. This was rejected by the Greek Cypriots, who wanted *enosis* or nothing. In 1950 Archbishop Makarios, newly appointed patriarch of the Orthodox Church on the island, placed himself at the head of a determined campaign for *enosis*. For Britain, Cyprus took on new strategic importance after the 1954 treaty with Egypt terminated Britain's right to her major military base at Suez. In 1955 Britain's Middle Eastern General Headquarters was moved to Cyprus. This was why, in July 1954, a minister in the Colonial Office said of Cyprus in the House of Commons, 'there are certain territories in the Commonwealth which, owing to their particular circumstances, can never expect to be fully independent' [4, 531 *col. 508*]. For Anthony Eden, Cyprus was vital: 'No Cyprus, no certain facilities to protect our supply of oil. No oil, unemployment and hunger in Britain' [32 *p. 364*].

Britain's clear determination to stay provoked the outbreak in April 1955 of a nationalist terrorist campaign designed to make the island ungovernable. It was led by a right-wing ex-army officer, George Grivas, who called his movement the National Organisation of Cypriot Fighters (EOKA). The British government found itself facing a typical imperial dilemma. Concessions to Greek Cypriot opinion would be denounced as appeasement by right-wing critics at home and risked angering Turkey, one of the lynchpins of the recently created Baghdad Pact. On the other hand, Labour Party opposition ensured that Cyprus became a domestic issue, and the Greek government's decision to refer the matter to the UN made it an international one. Under pressure from the UN, the British government called a conference in London in August 1955 to which it invited the governments of Greece and Turkey. Probably the British hoped that the conference would fail and that the reluctance of both Greece and Turkey to see the other gain control of Cyprus would provide them with a justification for remaining, which would be acceptable to the UN. At the conference Britain offered limited autonomy to the Cypriots, together with constitutional safeguards for the Turkish minority, but it broke up without agreement and EOKA stepped up their terrorist campaign. In September, Field Marshal Sir John Harding was appointed governor and given instructions to deal firmly with EOKA. Before long 25,000 British troops were tied down, chasing EOKA guerrillas numbered in hundreds. In March 1956 Makarios was arrested and imprisoned on the Seychelles. The cycle of terrorism and arbitrary justice continued on the island; Harding's efforts failed to destroy EOKA or even locate Grivas.

Macmillan reviewed Britain's Cyprus policy early in his premiership. On 15 March 1957 he wrote in his diary: 'I am as anxious as anyone to get clear of Cyprus. But I think we must try to reduce our liabilities in an orderly way. I am not persuaded that we need more than an airfield. . . . Then the Turks and Greeks could divide the rest of the island between them' [33 *p. 100*]. He took the decision to release Makarios, even though this cost him the resignation of Lord Salisbury, at the end of March. The 1957 Defence Review reduced the importance of Cyprus in favour of Kenya. In December Macmillan replaced Harding as governor with the more liberal Sir Hugh Foot, and in August 1958 he made a personal visit to Athens and Ankara to try to sell the Greek and Turkish governments his 'Tridominion' plan, by which each community would have its own legislature and British troops would remain for seven years, after which Turkey and Greece would divide the sovereignty of the island between them.

Macmillan's efforts were assisted by changes in the international climate and in Cyprus. The Suez Crisis and the Iraqi coup of 1958 destroyed the Baghdad Pact and made the Middle East more volatile and vulnerable to Soviet influence. Neither Greece nor Turkey wanted their NATO guarantee against the USSR put at risk by the Cyprus dispute. Serious riots between Greeks and Turks in Nicosia in 1958 had turned the EOKA campaign into a sectarian issue and, alarmed by the prospect of partition, Makarios publicly renounced *enosis* in September. Macmillan summoned another London conference in February 1959 at which agreement was reached. Cyprus would become independent in 1960 with a Greek president and a Turkish vice-president. The composition of the legislature would reflect the size of the two communities, and Britain would retain sovereign bases at Akrotiri and Dhekelia. All parties to the deal derived some satisfaction from it at the time, but inter-communal strife and the Turkish invasion of 1974 were to destroy the carefully calibrated constitutional balance of 1960.

The other Mediterranean island of strategic importance was Malta. It had achieved internal self-government in 1947, but its economic dependence on the British military base made it an unlikely candidate for dominion status. At a conference in 1955, even the possibility of Malta joining the United Kingdom and sending three MPs to Westminster was discussed. The scheme came to nothing, because a referendum on the island in February 1956 produced an inconclusive result and the British government had second thoughts about the cost of extending Britain's welfare system to Malta. The Defence Review of 1957 shifted Britain's strategic priorities from the Mediterranean to an 'east of Suez' policy and, with political opinion on the island increasingly in favour of independence, this was granted in September 1964.

Aden, commanding the entrance to the Red Sea, assumed a new importance for British overseas strategy after 1957, and especially after the independence of Kenya in 1960. The decision to develop Aden as a base coincided with the growth of Arab nationalism in the region and the predatory ambitions of neighbouring Yemen to gobble up the Aden Protectorate. Britain's response was similar to that produced elsewhere. She tried to construct a viable state by tying Aden to the neighbouring British-protected sheikhdoms in the Federation of South Arabia, created in 1963. Efforts to hand power to local conservatives coincided with suppression of Arab radicalism and intermittent intervention against the Nasserite revolutionaries in the Yemeni civil war which broke out in 1962. All of this increased the costs and difficulties of maintaining the base and made its value questionable.

Federation was also adopted in the West Indies, in an attempt to create a state large enough and wealthy enough to carry out colonial development programmes that would not be a constant drain on the British exchequer. The West Indian Federation came into existence in April 1958 but, in deference to the nationalism of the individual islands, its powers were weak. With its principal components – Jamaica and Trinidad – separated by 1,000 miles, it is not surprising that the centrifugal forces proved too strong. In August 1962, after a referendum, Jamaica left the Federation to become an independent member of the Commonwealth, as did Trinidad and Tobago.

In British Guiana on the South American mainland, the ethnic divisions were believed to be, in the words of the governor in 1950, 'an insuperable obstacle to complete self-government for some years to come' [98 *p. 245*]. The racial mixture of Guiana included Indians, Negroes, American Indians and various Europeans. Nevertheless, universal suffrage was introduced, but the election in April 1953 of a left-wing nationalist government of the People's Progressive Party (PPP), led by Dr Cheddi Jagan and drawing its support principally from the Indians, alarmed the other racial groups. In October, Britain, regarding Jagan as Marxist and sectarian, imposed a state of emergency backed by military might. The Colonial Secretary, Oliver Lyttelton, was confident that such gun-boat imperialism would not anger the United States and assured the Cabinet that 'anti-colonial sentiments would in this case be offset by anti-Communist sentiments' [98 *p. 249*]. He was right; by 1963 the Americans were even demanding that independence should be delayed until there was no risk of British Guiana going communist. Following a further electoral victory for the PPP in 1961, the British took advantage of a general strike in 1963 to alter the constitution and introduce proportional representation. This brought a more compliant regime to power, and British Guiana eventually became independent as Guyana in 1966.

Most, but not all, of the territories which became independent in the post-war period joined the British Commonwealth of Nations. To ensure that India did so, a neat constitutional formula had been devised in April 1949 to make republican government compatible with recognition of the British monarch as head of the Commonwealth. Britain hoped that the Commonwealth would develop into a third force in the world, to rival the USA and the USSR and preserve her global strategic and economic influence. This did not occur, because its members had little in common with one another and, with the decline of the Sterling Area, Britain was neither powerful enough nor influential enough to bind them together with anything more than sentiment. Also, there were rival attractions. In 1952 Australia and New Zealand tied their security to the United States in the ANZUS Pact, from which Britain was specifically excluded. In 1955 the Bandung Conference of Afro-Asian nations began the 'non-aligned' movement, which offered ex-colonial states an alternative to the Cold War division between West and East. As more countries joined the Commonwealth its diversity grew, and by 1960 there were doubts about whether it would survive. In 1961 South Africa became a republic and left the Commonwealth rather than face a chorus of criticism of its racial policies from other members. Macmillan's application to join the EEC suggested that by the early 1960s Britain had ceased to regard the Commonwealth as a vehicle for world influence or as a meaningful trading bloc. The word 'British' was dropped from its title in 1965 and the Commonwealth survives to this day as yet another international forum for the windy rhetoric of politicians and to provide the chance of a gold medal for athletes who would not win anything at the Olympics.

PART THREE: ASSESSMENT

5   THIRTEEN WASTED YEARS?

Like all governments, the Conservative administrations of 1951–64 attracted a good deal of contemporary criticism. Opposition to Britain's imperial withdrawal smouldered on the right wing of the Tory Party but never burst into open rebellion, and the Labour Party castigated the Conservatives' record as 'thirteen wasted years' during which the Tories had congratulated themselves on consumer affluence while ignoring Britain's fundamental economic problems. These governments, and Macmillan's in particular, have also attracted the opprobrium of Thatcherite politicians critical of the post-war consensus by which full employment, high welfare spending and the mixed economy were legitimate objects of Conservative policy, trade unions were appeased, and government spending and inflation allowed to grow. Historians and commentators have criticised the Tories for clinging to illusions about Britain's world status, her so-called special relationship with the United States, and the value and independence of her nuclear deterrent. As a result, Britain ignored the EEC at its inception and distorted her economy by investing too heavily in defence. Critics of the Tories' domestic record have seen it as governed by short-term considerations. The problems causing Britain's inexorable slide down the league table of international economic performance were not addressed because the pursuit of electoral success and crisis management dominated economic policy and tough decisions about issues such as trade-union reform and immigration were side-stepped. Macmillan's remark that 'most of our people have never had it so good' [33 *p. 64*] is so often quoted because it seems to sum up Tory complacency, even though it came in a speech in which he was warning about the fragility of consumer prosperity.

Much of this criticism is justified. The facts of Britain's economic decline are incontrovertible. Britain's growth rates lagged behind those of her main rivals, and her share of manufactured exports fell from 25.4 per cent in 1950 to 16.2 per cent in 1961 because her prices rose faster than those of her competitors [73]. The result was a series of balance-of-payments crises and regular bouts of international speculation against the pound. Inflationary pressures in a period of full employment made demands for wage rises hard to resist, and these contributed to the decline in productivity. The Conservatives have been criticised for lacking the will and the economic vision to break this downward spiral. British industry needed investment and modernisation, but instead the Tories consciously gave private consumption a higher priority than industrial reconstruction [12] and were reluctant to invest in industry – an area of employment that was regarded with contempt by Britain's public-school-educated elite. 'As late as 1961, the British state spent over £270m on aid to agriculture and less than £50m on industry and employment' [62 *p.* 273]. Furthermore, the Conservatives' policy of taxing profits and dividends higher than capital gains encouraged speculation in property rather than investment in industry. There was no attempt to confront the trade unions over the problems of over-manning and restrictive practices, nor was the secondary education system given the shake-up necessary to produce a flow of talented and trained recruits for industry [52]. Instead, the Tories were preoccupied with the short-term needs of their Stop-Go policy. Even this was badly managed, because fiscal and monetary levers were often applied after the worst of the problem had passed, and government policy reinforced the trend it was designed to counter [9; 53].

The policy of Stop-Go betrayed the confusion in Conservative economic thinking. Although committed to full employment, a mixed economy and a measure of Keynesian budgetary management, the party had not abandoned their traditional faith in free enterprise, low inflation, balanced budgets, a high-value pound and hostility to 'socialist' controls. The pursuit of sound money and low inflation was not easily reconciled with full employment, nor 'Tory freedom' with wage restraint; subsidies to agriculture clashed with free enterprise, while investment in nationalised industry implied a commitment to planning and control of the economy. Between 1951 and 1959 these contradictions were largely masked by the rising level of consumer affluence, which explains the Conservatives' successive electoral triumphs. In the early 1960s, with unemployment rising and inflation a persistent worry, the Conservatives tinkered with planning the economy, but failed to give Neddy or Nicky sufficient power to tackle the fundamental problems [62]. When, in 1963, de Gaulle closed the door to membership of the EEC as a route to greater economic prosperity, the Tories responded with a dash for growth that belied the party's traditional commitment to a high-value pound and a sound balance of payments.

Management of the nationalised industries provides an instructive example of the Conservatives' fuzzy economic thinking. Inflationary wage increases granted to some workers in nationalised industries in the early 1950s established the principle that the Treasury would subsidise loss-making public utilities [77]. The capital investment programmes for nationalised industries were susceptible to political control, which meant they received 'not the capital they needed, but the capital which the Treasury could spare from year to year' [73 *p. 312*]. This made it difficult for them to satisfy government demands that they should break even. Recognising that the nationalised industries 'have obligations of a national and non-economic kind' [73 *p. 312*], the Conservatives were reluctant to decide whether they were to be run as social services or commercial enterprises. Even Beeching's axe, designed to make the railways more profitable, was blunted by political pressures from marginal constituencies [70].

The determination of successive governments to maintain Britain's status as a world power has been blamed by some commentators for the nation's poor economic performance. Throughout the 1950s Britain devoted a higher proportion of GDP to defence spending than did any of her principal economic competitors, with the exception of the United States [81]. This not only had a harmful effect on the balance of payments but ensured that a disproportionate amount of Britain's research and development funds was gobbled up by the defence industries, whose work had few commercial spin-offs [12]. It was also an obsession with British governments that the value of the pound should remain high. Devaluation was out of the question, because it would undermine Britain's international status and the role of sterling as a reserve currency. This reinforced the Stop-Go cycle, because balance-of-payments crises could be cured only by doses of deflation which, by cutting back investment, progressively eroded the capacity of British industry to become more competitive.

There are some mitigating factors. Britain's economic decline did not begin in 1951, nor did it end in 1964. Both Attlee before and Wilson after them shared the Tories' assumptions about the need to maintain Britain's great-power status and defend the value of the pound. By cutting Britain's conventional forces the Tories succeeded in reducing defence spending as a proportion of GNP from 7.9 per cent in 1951 to 5.9 per cent in 1964 [93]. Compared with the inflation of the 1970s and the unemployment of the 1980s, the record of the Tory governments of the 1950s looks impressive. The pound lost 30 per cent of its value between 1951 and 1964, but 68 per cent in the following 13 years. Under the Tories in the 1950s unemployment never reached 900,000; since 1981 it has not been below 1.5 million [1]. To have streamlined Britain's archaic trade-union structure and modernised industrial management would have required a degree of interventionist control that was anathema to Conservative philosophy. In the 1950s it might well have proved politically suicidal; it would certainly have destroyed the sense of partnership between management and unions that governments were aiming to create. The Tories' record in controlling public-sector pay claims was reasonably good, but they had no power to control inflationary wage settlements that were made by private industries, confident that full employment ensured buoyant domestic demand for their products. Trade-union power could have been curbed only by severe deflation to create mass unemployment. This is precisely what the Tories, with their memories of the 1930s, were anxious to avoid.

Other aspects of their domestic policy have been criticised. Most commentators on Britain's twentieth-century decline have blamed the public schools for breeding a culture antithetical to industrial and entrepreneurial values. They argue that too many of the young men destined to dominate British society were taught to despise science, technology and commerce, and to aspire instead to careers in the professions or the armed forces [59; 84]. This problem dates back to the nineteenth century and was ignored by the Attlee governments, even though a report in 1944 had recommended closer integration between public schools and the state sector. It is not surprising that Conservative ministers, who were almost exclusively public-school products, did nothing about it. The affection for grammar schools among Tory voters explains why there was no reform of the secondary education system. However, the Conservatives can be credited for recognising the need for better technological education at tertiary level and expanding university education.

In castigating the Conservatives' record on industrial relations and immigration, Andrew Roberts has written that 'reactive politics characterized the liberal Toryism of the 1950s and 1960s. Prescience and pre-emptive action were always at a discount, and all too often sacrificed to short-term expediency and the craving for consensus'

[77 *pp. 222–3*]. But this is to ignore the context and assumptions of the day. As Edward Heath's government in the 1970s was to discover, industrial relations law which does not have the consent of the trade unions is doomed to fail without a background of mass unemployment. In the optimistic atmosphere of the 1950s, it was almost universally accepted that Keynesian demand-management had banished severe unemployment to the folk memories of the 1930s, and it is likely that any government presiding over its return would have been severely punished at the next election. Studies have shown that Britain's industrial relations compare favourably with her competitors, and it is arguable that the taming of trade-union power in the 1980s was achieved at too high a cost to Britain's manufacturing industries and social stability. The failure to legislate earlier on the problem of coloured immigration was not a weak-kneed capitulation to a difficult problem, but recognition of a genuine dilemma. Immigration became an issue at a time when hopes were high that the Commonwealth could be developed into a meaningful entity, and to have flouted opinion in the colonies and old dominions could have undermined those aspirations. Legislation would have been clearly discriminatory. While this might not have bothered right-wingers like Lord Salisbury, who wrote to a colleague, 'for me . . . it is a question whether great quantities of negroes . . . should be allowed to come' [7 *p. 301*], ministers' liberal attitudes are understandable at a time when colonial policy was trying to rein in the more extravagant claims made by white minorities in Britain's African territories.

With the benefit of hindsight it is easy to show that Britain's pretensions to be regarded as a world power were exposed as futile in the 1950s and that politicians should have adjusted their policies more radically to take account of her reduced status. The evidence was stark enough. Suez demonstrated Britain's inability to take unilateral action, of which the Americans disapproved, and by the early 1960s it was abundantly clear that Britain was being outstripped by her economic competitors and could no longer afford to produce her own nuclear weapons. Although they recognised that the Empire could not be maintained, politicians failed to draw the obvious conclusion that Britain no longer exercised global power. Even the Labour leader, Harold Wilson, a month after he became Prime Minister in October 1964 was proclaiming in his Mansion House speech: 'We are a world power and a world influence or we are nothing.' It can be argued that, in the 1950s, Britain took two wrong turnings. The first was her failure to join the EEC at its inception, and the second was Macmillan's dogged pursuit of the special relationship with the United States on which Britain's status as a nuclear power depended.

Scepticism about the potential of the EEC was understandable in 1955. Despite the success of the European Coal and Steel Community, the partnership of France and Germany appeared an unlikely basis on which the economic future of Europe could be built; only the previous year NATO unity had been threatened by French fears of German rearmament. Nor could Britain easily have abandoned her Commonwealth links in the mid-1950s. According to John Barnes:

> The proposal for a free-trade area, which was pushed by the Board of Trade under Thorneycroft once the decision not to join had been taken, and which Macmillan took up and pushed from the Treasury, was perhaps as far as any man could have taken Britain at that stage, and was in itself a radical proposal. [63 *p. 131*]

It may well be that, given de Gaulle's long-standing resentment and suspicion of Britain, her chances of joining the EEC were negligible once he had come to power in France in 1958, and that Macmillan's pro-American diplomacy only reinforced de Gaulle's determination to keep Britain out while providing him with the excuse to do so. This, however, does not entirely absolve Macmillan from blame for Britain's failure to join Europe. It had been on his advice as Chancellor that Britain accepted the Suez cease-fire. This decision reinforced the French suspicion that the British were American lackeys and destroyed the nascent Anglo-French entente that the crisis had created. Whether a Franco-British axis, keeping the Americans at arm's length, could have become the basis for economic and nuclear cooperation in Europe is an open question, but it suggests that there were alternatives to the policy that Macmillan adopted.

Britain's friendship with the United States was the cornerstone of Macmillan's foreign policy. The events of 1958 in the Middle East, in which both Britain and America intervened to shore up friendly regimes, vindicated him, since they demonstrated that Britain's overseas commitments could support American aims. Eisenhower's decision to allow Britain exclusive access to nuclear research secrets, and the Americans' eagerness to secure a British base for their nuclear submarines, suggested that the 'special relationship' was alive and well. However, the cancellation of Blue Streak in 1960, coinciding with the election of Kennedy to the White House, gave Macmillan's government an opportunity to abandon Britain's independent nuclear deterrent. The Americans made no secret of their hostility to it, the Russians had indicated that they regarded it as insignificant, and the cost of maintaining it could have been saved. This, though, was unthinkable to the Macmillan administration. The Defence White Paper of 1957 had underlined the importance of nuclear weapons to Britain's strategic planning, and Macmillan was determined to secure an American replacement for Blue Streak – first Skybolt and then Polaris. The deal struck with Kennedy at Nassau in December 1962 gave Britain little more than token independence. Although Britain could fire her Polaris missiles in defence of her 'supreme national interests' [66 *p. 316*], it was inconceivable that this would happen independently of NATO. The strategic value of continuing to be a nuclear power was negligible, but Macmillan did ̧achieve some political capital from it. Britain remained one of an exclusive club of five nuclear powers, and this undoubtedly helped him to act as broker to the Test Ban Treaty of 1963.

Although they clung to the great-power status seemingly conferred by the possession of nuclear weapons, the Conservative governments of the 1950s adopted a much more realistic and pragmatic attitude to the Empire. They took office hopeful that the process of granting colonial independence could be so managed as to preserve informal British power through the Sterling Area, regional defence agreements and membership of the Commonwealth. The difficulties of remaining in control of colonial nationalism once the moves towards self-government and eventual independence had begun forced them to abandon some of these aspirations, especially as the international situation altered markedly in the second half of the decade. Although historians are divided over whether the Suez Crisis accelerated Britain's withdrawal from Africa [117], it certainly contributed to an international climate increasingly hostile to European colonialism and in which Third World powers were more confident about challenging the hegemony of the United States and the Soviet Union. It is to the credit of Macmillan's government that it recognised and accepted these trends, even if its colonial policy laid it open to charges, at the time and later, of withdrawing too hastily from the Empire and thereby contributing to the violent instability of post-colonial African politics. Macmillan himself was aware of this danger. In his memoirs he recalls being told by a colonial governor that a particular colony would not be ready for freedom for 15 to 20 years but that independence should still be granted immediately because the alternative was rebellion and repression [38 *pp. 118–19*]. This advice clearly influenced the acceleration of colonial independence that occurred from 1960 and, despite the unfortunate legacy in some places, it is hard to dispute Iain Macleod's verdict that 'there were risks in moving quickly. But the risks of moving slowly were far greater' [7 *p. 571*].

The legacy of the Conservative governments from 1951 to 1964 is mixed. While vulnerable to the charge that their economic and domestic policies were too much preoccupied with short-term considerations to the detriment of Britain's long-term future, they presided over a society that was less divided and less prone to the ravages of inflation and high unemployment than it later became. Of course, this may have been more the result of prevailing world conditions than of government economic policy or the commitment to consensus that dominated the decade, but there was real progress and change in British society during the 1950s. If overseas and defence policy was tinged with delusions of grandeur, the Tories of the 1950s were not unique among British governments for this, and they showed a remarkable capacity to adapt to rapidly changing circumstances. The Tories left office in 1964 at a time when traditional British values and institutions were subject to unprecedented scrutiny and criticism. They were derided by contemporary critics as anachronistic and incompetent, but the passage of time allows historians to judge them more judiciously and dispassionately.

PART FOUR: DOCUMENTS

DOCUMENT 1 THE CONSERVATIVES IN OPPOSITION

While in opposition, the Conservative Party reviewed its philosophy, organisation and tactics. R.A. Butler was a key figure in the process.

Our first purpose was to counter the charge and the fear that we were the party of industrial go-as-you-please and devil-take-the-hindmost, that full employment and the Welfare State were not safe in our hands. We therefore took our cue ... from the existing complexity of modern industry and Britain's position as a debtor country which made reversion to *laissez-faire* impossible. ... The Charter was ... first and foremost an assurance that, in the interests of efficiency, full employment and social security, modern Conservatism would maintain strong central guidance over the operation of the economy.

Our second purpose was to present a recognizable alternative to the reigning orthodoxies of socialism – not to put the clock back, but to reclaim a prominent role for individual initiative and private enterprise in the mixed and managed economy. ... What stands out very plainly is the extent to which we foresaw and foreshadowed the characteristically Conservative measures of the post-1951 period. ... Our imperative need was to establish what was then very far from being taken for granted: the Conservative intention to reconcile individual effort with a proper measure of central planning and direction and, no less important, to 'point to a way of life designed to free private endeavour from the taint of selfishness or self-interest' ...

This brings me to our third purpose which was, quite simply, to make a new approach to the adjustment of human relations within industry. We offered to the worker a charter of rights giving assurance of steady employment, incentive to test his ability to the utmost, and status as an individual personality. Though we were persuaded that such a charter could not be made the subject of an Act of Parliament ... what chiefly concerned the Industrial Policy Committee was the need to strengthen by example and precept the channels of communication and co-operation between management and workers.

Lord Butler, [21], pp. 146–7

DOCUMENT 2   CRITICISM OF ANTHONY EDEN'S LEADERSHIP

On 3 January 1956 The Daily Telegraph – a paper which normally supported the Conservatives – carried an article by deputy editor Donald McLachlan bemoaning Eden's lack of leadership. The article influenced Eden's decision to take a tough line in the Suez Crisis later that year.

Why are the men who triumphed at the polls last May now under a cloud of disfavour with their own supporters? Why are Conservatives around the country restive, and Ministers and backbenchers unenraptured with their leader? ...

There is a favourite gesture of the Prime Minister's which is sometimes recalled to illustrate this sense of disappointment. To emphasise a point he will clench one fist to smack the open palm of the other hand – but the smack is seldom heard. Most Conservatives, and almost certainly some of the wiser trade union leaders, are waiting to feel the smack of firm government ...

The actual criticisms ... fall under three heads: changes of mind by the Government; half-measures; and the postponement of decisions ...

In a very few months the Government, although confronted with a divided Labour party in a tame House of Commons, has lost prestige and repute. A collection of able men, with plenty of ideas before them and administrative experience behind them, have failed to develop the cohesion and thrust of a good team. ... The spirit and the strategy can be created only by the Prime Minister himself.

The Daily Telegraph, 3 January 1956.

DOCUMENT 3   THE PROFUMO AFFAIR

On 11 June 1963, a week after Profumo's resignation and six days before the Commons debate on the affair, The Times published a leader under the headline, 'It is a moral issue'. The article claimed that the Profumo Affair was symptomatic of Britain's decadence after a decade of Conservative rule. It was also seen as a call to Conservative MPs to have Macmillan replaced as Prime Minister.

Eleven years of Conservative rule have brought the nation psychologically and spiritually to a low ebb. The Conservatives came to power a few months before the present reign opened. They have been in office so far throughout the whole of it. The ardent hopes and eager expectations that attended its beginning have been belied. ... Nothing else, they seemed later to think, mattered, compared with the assertion that the nation had never had it so good. Today they are faced with a flagging economy, an uncertain future, and the end of the illusion that Britain's greatness could be measured by the so-called independence of its so-called deterrent. All this may seem far from Mr Profumo, but his admissions could be the last straw ...

The Prime Minister and his colleagues can cling together and still be there a year hence. They will have to do more than that to justify themselves ...

There are plenty of earnest and serious men in the Conservative Party who know that all is not well. It is time they put first things first, stopped weighing electoral chances, and returned to the starker truths of an earlier day. Popularity by affluence is about played out, especially when it rests on so insecure a basis.

The Times, 11 June 1963.

DOCUMENT 4   MACMILLAN'S RESIGNATION

This article by Iain Macleod described Macmillan's determination to prevent Butler succeeding him as Prime Minister in October 1963. The intrigue, and Macleod's article, discredited the system by which the Conservatives chose their leader.

At all times, from the first day of his Premiership to the last, Macmillan was determined that Butler, although incomparably the best qualified of the contenders, should not succeed him. ... He thought ... that Butler had not in him the steel that makes a Prime Minister, nor the inspiration that a Leader needs to pull his party through a fierce general election ...

That Butler is mystifying, complex and sometimes hard to approach I would concede. But, on the other hand, he has the priceless quality of being able to do any job better than you think he will, and of attracting to himself wide understanding support from many people outside the Tory Party. And without such an appeal no general election can be won ...

It is some measure of the tightness of the magic circle on this occasion that neither the Chancellor of the Exchequer [Maudling] nor the Leader of the House of Commons [Macleod] had any inkling of what was happening ...

I told him [Home] that there was no one in the party for whom I had more admiration and respect; that if he had been in the House of Commons he could perhaps have been the first choice; but I felt that those giving advice had grossly underestimated the difficulties of presenting the situation in a convincing way to the modern Tory Party. Unlike Hailsham, he was not a reluctant peer, and we were now proposing to admit that after twelve years of Tory government no one amongst the 363 members of the party in the House of Commons was acceptable as Prime Minister ...

Iain Macleod, writing in *The Spectator*, 17 January 1964.

DOCUMENT 5   INDUSTRIAL RELATIONS UNDER THE
              TORIES

*Anthony Eden described why the Tories were reluctant to introduce
legislation on industrial relations.*

I discussed the situation with Sir Walter Monckton and one or two senior
colleagues and decided upon a general review of industrial relations. The
talks which I had held at 10 Downing Street during the strikes had made
some things clear. The trade union leaders saw the dangers and they were
concerned at the indiscipline among some union members, which was aimed
in part at them. If the Government could strengthen their hand, they would
welcome it, but they did not want any fresh legislation. I had not much
faith in this either.

The employers were much concerned to avoid action which would
precipitate a collision with the unions. The climate for agreement was
therefore pretty good. I wanted to use it to determine policy in advance of
the next round of trouble. There were too many unofficial strikes; the
question was whether these should be made illegal. Both sides of industry
were opposed to this and I shared their doubts as to whether legislation
would be effective. Everybody would be in a worse position if it were not.
We canvassed the proposal that a secret ballot should be made compulsory
before any union took strike action. This had many supporters, but it would
be difficult to supervise and would not prevent unofficial strikes. We also
considered means of extending the existing system of arbitration, but these
could hardly be made effective without a general independent inquiry into
industrial relations, a slow business and no immediate solution.

Sir Anthony Eden, [27], pp. 286–7.

DOCUMENT 6   THE IMMIGRATION ISSUE

*Although the scale of immigration from the new Commonwealth began to
worry ministers in the mid-1950s, legislation was not introduced.*

The Cabinet had before them a memorandum by the Home Secretary ...
covering a draft of a Bill to control the entry into the United Kingdom of
British subjects from overseas and discussing the issues which would have to
be settled before such legislation could be introduced ...
   In discussion the following points were made:-
   (a) The problem of Colonial immigration had not yet aroused general
public anxiety, although there was some concern, mainly due to housing
difficulties, in a few localities where most of the recent immigrants were
concentrated. On the other hand, if immigration from the Colonies, and, for

that matter, from India and Pakistan, were allowed to continue unchecked, there was a real danger that over the years there would be a significant change in the racial character of the English people.

(b) All the Colonies had power to control the immigration of British subjects into their territories. They should not regard it as unreasonable if the United Kingdom took power to apply similar restrictions. As against this it was argued that such a step would be inconsistent with the traditional policy that British subjects should have the right of free entry into the Mother country of the Commonwealth, and would be widely regarded as an illiberal development.

(c) On economic grounds immigration, including Colonial immigration, was a welcome means of augmenting our labour resources. It was the condition of full employment here that was attracting these immigrants. The Trades Union Congress were, in general, averse to the imposition of restrictions on Colonial immigration, although individual Unions might well take a different line.

(d) If powers were to be taken to control the entry of British subjects from overseas, it seemed desirable that similar restrictions should be applied to citizens of the Irish Republic. But, apart from the fact that we needed Irish labour, it would be impracticable to control immigration from the Irish Republic without applying restrictions to travel between Great Britain and Northern Ireland.

(e) Consideration might be given to the possibility of admitting Colonial immigrants for temporary employment for a period not exceeding five years. This might meet the present need for labour with less prejudice to long-term social conditions.

The Prime Minister, summing up the discussion, said that it was evident that further thought must be given to this problem before the Cabinet could decide whether legislation should be introduced ...

Cabinet Minutes, 3 November 1955. PRO CAB 128/29.

DOCUMENT 7   **THE LABOUR PARTY'S DIFFICULTIES ON THE ISSUE OF IMMIGRATION**

The Labour Party was opposed in principle to legislation on coloured immigration, but found many of its working-class supporters in favour. Its spokesmen were cautious and equivocal on the issue.

I don't think that at the moment the rate of immigration of coloured people ... has reached the point where there should yet be this sort of control. ... But I ... would not reject the idea of control, as such. I would be very reluctant to impose it; I think it's extremely important for the survival of the Commonwealth ... that we should not control immigration from other parts

of the Commonwealth unless it becomes absolutely necessary to do so. I
don't think it is yet necessary.

Patrick Gordon-Walker, speaking on the radio, 31 August 1961.

DOCUMENT 8   GAITSKELL'S ATTEMPT TO REVISE
                CLAUSE FOUR

*Gaitskell believed that commitment to Clause Four nationalisation had
contributed significantly to the Labour Party's defeat in the 1959 general
election.*

We have to show ... that we are a modern mid-twentieth century party,
looking to the future, not to the past. ... There seems no doubt that, if we
are to accept the majority view of those who fought this election,
nationalisation – on balance – lost us votes. ... What the voters disliked was
not so much our policy but what they came to think our policy was. Our
moderate, practical proposals were distorted out of all recognition by our
opponents. ... The Party Constitution [was] written over 40 years ago. It
seems to me that this needs to be brought up to date. ... It implies that we
propose to nationalise everything, but do we? Everything? – the whole of
light industry, the whole of agriculture, all the shops – every little pub and
garage? Of course not. We have long ago come to accept, we know very
well, for the foreseeable future, at least in some form, a mixed economy; in
which case, if this is our view – as I believe it to be of 90 per cent of the
Labour Party, had we better not say so instead of going out of our way to
court misrepresentation? ... I am sure that the Webbs and Arthur
Henderson who largely drafted this Constitution, would have been amazed
and horrified had they thought that their words were to be treated as
sacrosanct 40 years later in utterly changed conditions.

Gaitskell's speech to the Labour Party Conference at Blackpool, November
1959.

DOCUMENT 9   HAROLD WILSON IN 1960

*In November 1960 Wilson challenged Gaitskell for the leadership of the
Labour Party, presenting himself as the man to unite the party after
Gaitskell's divisive campaign to reform Clause Four. To some of his
colleagues, however, Wilson's move was no more than a piece of cynical
opportunism.*

I had got Harold Wilson to come and pick me up and it was obvious that he was desperately worried. Poor little man, he has really cornered himself this time. He knew he would be pressed to stand against Hugh, in which case he would be committing political suicide, and he wants to stand as Deputy Leader instead. But he also knows that, if he doesn't stand against Hugh, he will be accused of cowardice and he may well be defeated for Deputy Leader, now George Brown has jumped on the bandwagon again and has Hugh's backing. Here is an object lesson in the master-tactician and the super-opportunist, who is so clever that his tactics are disastrous and he destroys his opportunities. But what can I say about somebody who, throughout all these talks, has been utterly trivial, complacent and vain?

Richard Crossman, [41], p. 880. 13 October 1960.

DOCUMENT 10   WILSON'S SCIENTIFIC PANACEA

Harold Wilson was able to present the Labour Party as modern and dynamic by uniting it behind his call for the development of science and technology as the key to future economic success.

We are living perhaps in a more rapid revolution than some of us realise. The period of 15 years from the last time we were in Scarborough, in 1960, to the middle of the 1970s will embrace a period of technical change, particularly in industrial methods, greater than in the whole industrial revolution of the last 250 years ...

Unless we can harness science to our economic planning, we are not going to get the expansion that we need. What is needed is structural changes in British industry ...

We are re-defining and we are re-stating our Socialism in terms of the scientific revolution. ... The Britain that is going to be forged in the white heat of this revolution will be no place for restrictive practices or for outdated methods on either side of industry ...

Because we care deeply about the future of Britain, we must use all the resources of democratic planning, all the latent and underdeveloped energies and skills of our people, to ensure Britain's standing in the world.

Harold Wilson's speech to the Labour Party Conference at Scarborough, October 1963.

DOCUMENT 11   MR BUTSKELL

The Economist invented the figure of Mr Butskell, to suggest that Butler's policies as Chancellor were no different from those of his Labour predecessor, Gaitskell.

Mr. Butskell is already a well-known figure in dinner table conversations in both Westminster and Whitehall, and the time has come to introduce him to a wider audience. He is a composite of the present Chancellor and the previous one. ... Whenever there is a tendency to excess conservatism within the Conservative party – such as a clamour for too much imperial preference, for a wild dash to convertibility, or even for a little more unemployment to teach the workers a lesson – Mr. Butskell speaks up for the cause of moderation from the Government side of the House; when there is a clamour for even graver irresponsibilities from the Labour benches, Mr. Butskell has hitherto spoken up from the other. ... He is willing to bolster up demand when there is slack in the economy, or to trim down demand a little (a very little) when there is a danger of inflation. But – and this is the secret – he has not yet shown himself to be a really strong character in the face of adversity; political pressures stand in his way. If ever external economic events make it necessary to cut down demand very ruthlessly, he is quite likely to run away.

The Economist, 13 February 1954.

DOCUMENT 12   THE ECONOMIC SITUATION IN 1951

In October 1951 the new Chancellor, R.A. Butler, painted a depressing picture of the state of Britain's economy to the incoming Conservative government.

I wish to put before my colleagues an analysis of the present economic position of the United Kingdom, as evidenced in our Balance of Payments with the dollar area and the rest of the world.

We are in a balance of payments crisis, worse than 1949, and in many ways worse even than 1947. Confidence in sterling is impaired and speculation against it is considerable, increasing the deficits and the drain on our gold and dollar reserves ...

This very serious deterioration in our position, coming as it does at the inception and not during the full impact of the rearmament programme, threatens the whole position of sterling and of the United Kingdom and sterling area. It is a clear indication not only that there are serious underlying weaknesses in our position, but also that foreign confidence in our ability to deal with these weaknesses is greatly impaired ...

Cabinet Memorandum, 31 October 1951. PRO CAB 129/48.

DOCUMENT 13   THORNEYCROFT'S DEFLATIONARY POLICIES

Macmillan's first Chancellor, Peter Thorneycroft, was more concerned about the risks of inflation than his Prime Minister. In October 1957 he outlined a package of deflationary measures to Parliament. Three months later he resigned from the government in opposition to Macmillan's economic policies.

The purpose of the measures is to limit the availability of money; to serve notice on ourselves and on the world outside that we are no longer prepared to underwrite, through the banking system or through spending by the Government, the consequences of inflationary actions. ... I have asked the banks to control money supplies as in the public sector by placing a limit on the amount of money that they provide. ... In our present situation, we need to limit the money supply, and no purpose, however good, must outweigh that objective. ... The measures we have taken in relation to the money supplies are intended to make it harder both to earn profits and to get wage increases. They will operate over a wide area. ... It is indeed, certain, that one cause of inflation since the war has been the attempt to drive the economy at a pace above and beyond what can be justified by our resources of men, money and materials. But the truth about unemployment is this: without the measures we have announced there would have been massive unemployment within a matter of months. We depend on the value of our pound to buy our food and our raw materials and a stable pound is the prerequisite of full employment. We must, therefore, put it first. Of course, other policies will be urged; appeals for restraint and the whole armoury of physical controls. But those controls have been tried before. They have been tried with all the machinery of control in full existence and inherited from a major world war, and even then they failed. Some economists are urging us to spend our way out of the present difficulty, and that sounds a most attractive remedy indeed, but I do not believe it is one which will be adopted by the common sense of the House of Commons. In any event, it proposes no remedy for rising prices.

Thorneycroft's statement to Parliament, 29 October 1957, [4], 575, cols 51–58.

DOCUMENT 14   THE FORMATION OF NEDDY AND NICKY

In his memoirs, Macmillan described his response to the economic difficulties of the early 1960s.

At the end of July 1961 the Treasury, supported or instigated by the Bank of England, had become seriously alarmed at the continued signs of inflation now reflected in an unfavourable balance of payments for the third year in succession. Although I was temperamentally opposed to some of the deflationary proposals which the 'authorities' seemed to think necessary, I was forced to agree to certain further measures of restriction. These involved new economies in public expenditure and more rigorous exchange control as well as deflationary steps calculated to curtail consumption, including the temporary raising of the Bank Rate to seven per cent ...

The pay pause of 1961–2 was the first – no doubt amateurish – attempt to move towards what has afterwards become known as an 'incomes policy'. Since the concept was novel, and the leaders of the trade unions in Britain are conspicuous for their conservatism, the pay pause not unnaturally resulted in serious political difficulties and pressures as well as the prospect of widespread conflict involving bitter opposition to the Government of the day ...

Meanwhile, the Chancellor of the Exchequer and I worked on a letter to be addressed to both sides of industry proposing the creation of the National Economic Development Council, drawn from trade unions, management and government who would participate in central planning advice. ... This institution, now commonly known as 'Neddy', has become an important and valuable part of our national machinery. ... Wages and wage demands seemed to be growing every day. ... One of the usual symptoms of a boom, that is unjustified wage demands, continued unchecked. For this unexpected persistence of high fever in spite of a low diet, a new term of art was later devised – 'stagflation'. ... I seemed to get little support from the practitioners of most repute, who appeared satisfied with the traditional forms of febrifuge – blood-letting, purging and the rest. I was therefore thrown back either on quack doctors or on an attempt, amid many other pre-occupations, to devise some new treatment by my own efforts.

[Macmillan then quoted his diary.] I have been trying to work on 'Incomes Policy: A New Approach'. There is a mass of paper and a large number of suggestions (mostly self-contradictory). ... We are making some progress with Incomes Policy ...

We made a start with a new form of these proposals (especially for the National Commission on Wages and Salaries) and with some of the other plans. It will now be necessary, with the help of the Treasury, Board of Trade, and Minister of Labour to produce a paper for the Cabinet to approve (or disapprove).

Harold Macmillan, [39], pp. 35–7, 85–6.

DOCUMENT 15   EDEN'S ASSESSMENT OF BRITAIN'S ROLE

In common with British governments before them, the Conservatives found themselves having to meet huge overseas obligations with dwindling resources. Eden recommended that Britain should try to share her burdens with the USA.

4. It is becoming clear that rigorous maintenance of the presently-accepted policies of Her Majesty's Government at home and abroad is placing a burden on the country's economy which it is beyond the resources of the country to meet. A position has already been reached where there is no reserve and therefore no margin for unforeseen additional obligations.

5. The first task must be to determine how far the external obligations of the country can be reduced or shared with others, or transferred to other shoulders, without impairing too seriously the world position of the United Kingdom and sacrificing the vital advantages which flow from it. But if, after careful review, it is shown that the total effort required is still beyond the capacity of existing national resources, a choice of the utmost difficulty lies before the British people, for they must either give up, for a time, some of the advantages which a high standard of living confers upon them, or, by relaxing their grip in the outside world, see their country sink to the level of a second-class Power, with injury to their essential interests and way of life of which they can have little conception. Faced with this choice, the British people might be rallied to a greater productive effort which would enable a greater volume of external commitments to be borne ...

28. It is apparent from this review that there are few ways to effect any reductions in our overseas commitments which would provide immediate relief to our economic difficulties ...

29. If, on a longer view, it must be assumed that the maintenance of the present scale of overseas commitments will permanently overstrain our economy, clearly we ought to recognise that the United Kingdom is over-committed and must reduce the commitment. The only practical way of removing this permanent strain would be for the United Kingdom to shed or share the load of one or two major obligations e.g. the defence of the Middle East, for which at present we bear the responsibility alone, or the defence of South-East Asia, where we share responsibility with the French. Our present policy is in fact directed towards the construction of international defence organisations for the Middle East and South-East Asia in which the United States and other Commonwealth countries would participate. Our aim should be to persuade the United States to assume the real burdens in such organisations, while retaining for ourselves as much political control – and hence prestige and world influence – as we can ...

30. The success of this policy will depend on a number of factors, some

favourable, some unfavourable. The United States is the only single country in the free world capable of assuming new and world-wide obligations; being heavily committed to the East–West struggle they would not readily leave a power-vacuum in any part of the globe but would be disposed, however reluctantly, to fill it themselves if it was clear that the United Kingdom could no longer hold the position (as they did, for example, in Greece). On the other hand ... distrust of the British and fear of becoming an instrument to prop up a declining British Empire are still strong. ... As regards the United Kingdom part, a policy of this kind will only be successful with the United States in so far as we are able to demonstrate that we are making the maximum possible effort ourselves, and the more gradually and inconspicuously we can transfer the real burdens from our own to American shoulders, the less damage we shall do to our position and influence in the world.

'British Overseas Obligations'. Cabinet Memorandum by the Foreign Secretary, 18 June 1952. PRO CAB 129/53.

DOCUMENT 16   THE BRITISH CABINET'S REACTION TO THE SUEZ CRISIS

Nasser's nationalisation of the Suez Canal on 26 July 1956 posed the British government a number of problems.

The Cabinet agreed that we should be on weak ground in basing our resistance on the narrow argument that Colonel Nasser had acted illegally. The Suez Canal Company was registered as an Egyptian company under Egyptian law; and Colonel Nasser had indicated that he intended to compensate the shareholders at ruling market price. From a narrow legal point of view, his action amounted to no more than a decision to buy out the shareholders. Our case must be presented on wider international grounds. Our argument must be that the Canal was an important international asset and facility, and that Egypt could not be allowed to exploit it for a purely internal purpose. The Egyptians had not the technical ability to manage it effectively; and their recent behaviour gave no confidence that they would recognise their international obligations in respect of it. ... It was not a piece of Egyptian property but an international asset of the highest importance and it should be managed as an international trust.

The Cabinet agreed that for these reasons every effort must be made to restore effective international control over the Canal. It was evident that the Egyptians would not yield to economic pressures alone. They must be subjected to the maximum political pressure which could be applied by the maritime and trading nations whose interests were most directly affected. And, in the last resort, this political pressure must be backed by the threat – and, if need be, the use – of force.

The fundamental question before the Cabinet, however, was whether they were prepared in the last resort to pursue their objective by the threat or even the use of force, and whether they were ready, in default of assistance from the United States and France, to take military action alone.

The Cabinet agreed that our essential interests in this area must, if necessary, be safeguarded by military action and that the necessary preparations to this end must be made. Failure to hold the Suez Canal would lead inevitably to the loss one by one of all our interests and assets in the Middle East and, even if we had to act alone, we could not stop short of using force to protect our position if all other means of protecting it proved unavailing . . .

British Cabinet Minutes, 27 July 1956, [87], p. 133.

DOCUMENT 17   EISENHOWER DISAGREES WITH EDEN
                OVER SUEZ

President Eisenhower, although he sympathised with Eden's hostility to Nasser, did not believe that the Suez issue should be resolved by force.

If the diplomatic front we present is united and is backed by the overwhelming sentiment of our several peoples, the chances should be greater that Nasser will give way without the need for any resort to force ...

I am afraid, Anthony, that from this point onward our views on this situation diverge. ... I regard it as indispensable that if we are to proceed solidly together to the solution of this problem, public opinion in our several countries must be overwhelming in its support. I must tell you frankly that American public opinion flatly rejects the thought of using force, particularly when it does not seem that every possible peaceful means of protecting our vital interests has been exhausted without result ...

I really do not see how a successful result could be achieved by forcible means. The use of force would, it seems to me, vastly increase the area of jeopardy. I do not see how the economy of Western Europe can long survive the burden of prolonged military operations, as well as the denial of Near East oil. Also the peoples of the Near East and of North Africa and, to some extent, of all of Asia and all of Africa, would be consolidated against the West to a degree which, I fear, could not be overcome in a generation, and perhaps not even in a century, particularly having in mind the capacity of the Russians to make mischief ...

We have friends in the Middle East who tell us they would like to see Nasser's deflation brought about. But they seem unanimous in feeling that the Suez is not the issue on which to attempt to do this by force. Under those circumstances, because of the temper of their population, they say they would have to support Nasser even against their better judgment.

Eisenhower's letter to Eden, 2 September 1956, [87], p. 119.

DOCUMENT 18   **THE SEVRES PROTOCOL**

On 24 October 1956, government representatives from Britain, France and Israel signed a secret agreement to coordinate their attacks on Egypt.

The results of the conversations which took place at Sèvres from 22nd–24th October 1956 between the representatives of the Governments of the United Kingdom, the State of Israel and of France are the following:

1. The Israeli forces launch in the evening of 29th October 1956 a large scale attack on the Egyptian forces with the aim of reaching the Canal zone the following day.

2. On being apprised of these events, the British and French Governments during the day of 30th October 1956 respectively and simultaneously make two appeals to the Egyptian Government and the Israeli Government on the following lines:
A. To the Egyptian Government:
   (a) halt all acts of war;
   (b) withdraw all its troops ten miles from the Canal;
   (c) accept temporary occupation of key positions on the Canal by the Anglo-French forces to guarantee freedom of passage through the Canal by vessels of all nations until a final settlement.
B. To the Israeli Government:
   (a) halt all acts of war;
   (b) withdraw all its troops ten miles to the east of the Canal.
In addition, the Israeli Government will be notified that the French and British Governments have demanded of the Egyptian Government to accept temporary occupation of key positions along the Canal by Anglo-French forces.
   It is agreed that if one of the Governments refused, or did not give its consent, within twelve hours the Anglo-French forces would intervene with the means necessary to ensure that their demands are accepted.
C.   That representatives of the three Governments agree that the Israeli Government will not be required to meet the conditions in the appeal addressed to it, in the event that the Egyptian Government does not accept those in the appeal addressed to it for their part.

3. In the event that the Egyptian Government should fail to agree within the stipulated time to the conditions of the appeal addressed to it, the Anglo-French forces will launch military operations against the Egyptian forces in the early hours of the morning of 31st October.

4. The Israeli Government will send forces to occupy the western shore of the Gulf of Akaba and the group of islands Tirane and Sanafir to ensure freedom of navigation in the Gulf of Akaba.

5. Israel undertakes not to attack Jordan during the period of operations against Egypt. But in the event that during the same period Jordan should attack Israel, the British Government undertakes not to come to the aid of Jordan.

6. The arrangements of the present protocol must remain strictly secret.

7. They will enter into force after the agreement of the three Governments. (signed) David Ben Gurion, Patrick Dean, Christian Pineau.

Kyle, [109], pp. 565–7.

DOCUMENT 19   EDEN AND COLLUSION

Eden denied that his government had colluded with the Israelis.

We have been accused of being, ever since the Israeli attack on Egypt, and indeed long before that, in collusion with the Israelis. My right hon. and learned friend the Foreign Secretary emphatically denied that charge on 31st October. Since then, it seems that the charge has been altered and Her Majesty's Government have been asked to prove that they had no foreknowledge of the Israeli attack ...

To say – and this is what I want to repeat to the House – that Her Majesty's Government were engaged in some dishonourable conspiracy is completely untrue, and I most emphatically deny it ...

I want to say this on the question of foreknowledge, and to say it quite bluntly to the House, that there was not foreknowledge that Israel would attack Egypt – there was not.

Eden's statements to the House of Commons, 20 December 1956, [4], 562, cols 1457–58 and 1518.

DOCUMENT 20   **POPULAR REACTIONS TO THE SUEZ CRISIS**

A selection of letters sent by members of the public to Conservative Central Office.

(a) I strongly support Sir Anthony Eden's action during the past few days in dealing with Nasser and the Egyptian 'Wogs' (I served during the war with the RAF and know of the Egyptians). ... People such as myself who cannot claim to be true Tories (though recent events are

helping to make me one) view the Labour Party with alarm. ... Having just watched the late night news on ITV watching Labour supporters or rather mobsters attempting to storm Downing Street, I can only feel sick with disgust for the opposition.
S.C. of Edgware, Middlesex, 4 November 1956.

(b) We have supported your party for many years, and in this family there are at present seven votes – but we have all decided that in future we just cannot vote for Mr. Eden. This last few days has been dreadful for us all and we have all had to make this decision most reluctantly. I may add that we are not against doing our bit – in the 1914–18 job I was in the Guards and my eldest son was in the same Regt in the last war – but we just cannot see sense or reason in this present dreadful affair.
C.E.C. of Gayton Thorpe, King's Lynn, 6 November 1956.

(c) For your information. In the past I have voted as I thought – *sane* Labour. I am now like many thousands more determined to vote *Blue*. ... Please treat this confidentially. As I am only one of the Old Contemptibles, consequently not much use. But will watch where I will put my X the next time.
W.S. of Ashton-under-Lyme, Lancashire, 26 November 1956.

Conservative Party archives, Bodleian Library, Oxford CCO 4/7/135–141.

DOCUMENT 21   MACMILLAN'S GRAND DESIGN

At the end of 1960 Macmillan composed a long memorandum in which he reflected on the difficulty of accommodating de Gaulle without compromising Britain's special relationship with the USA.

13.   ... By a strange paradox, if de Gaulle were to disappear, an accommodation might be ... more difficult. Whatever happened in France, there would be great confusion, perhaps even disintegration. French Federalist opinion would be strengthened (Monnet and all that) and timid Frenchmen would seek a refuge in a European Federal State. Difficult as de Gaulle is, his view of the proper *political* structure (Confederation not Federation) is really nearer to ours. If he wished us to join the political institutions it would be easier for us to do so if they took the form which he favours ...

14. We ought therefore to make a supreme effort to reach a settlement while de Gaulle is in power in France. ... Why is he obstructing a

settlement? How are we to do a deal with him? I am sure that a settlement can only be reached on political lines. Sixes and Sevens (in spite of all the difficulties and complications – G.A.T.T. and all that) is now not primarily an economic but a political problem and should be dealt with as such ...

25. What do we want?
 What does de Gaulle want?
 How far can we agree to help him if he will help us?
 (a) *We want Sixes and Sevens settled.*
 We must make it clear to the French that we mean what we say – that if it is *not* settled, Europe will be divided politically and militarily ...
 (b) *De Gaulle wants the recognition of France as a Great Power, at least equal to Britain.*
 He suspects the Anglo-Saxons.
So long as the 'Anglo-Saxon domination' continues, he will not treat Britain as European, but as American – a junior partner of America, but a partner ...
De Gaulle feels that ... the vital decisions are made – or not made – between the American and British Governments in Washington. De Gaulle feels that he is *excluded* from this club or partnership. Hence –
 (a) his persistent efforts towards 'Tripartitism' – which the Americans and the British have accepted 'en principe' to a limited extent, but have never really operated;
 (b) his determination – whatever the cost – that France should become a *nuclear* power. For it is France's *exclusion* from the nuclear club that is the measure of France's inferior status. It is particularly galling for him that Britain should have an independent nuclear capacity; he accepts that the United States is in a different category.
 Can what *we* want and what *de Gaulle* wants be brought into harmony? Is there a basis for a deal? ...

30. ... Can we give him our techniques, or our bombs, or any share of *our* nuclear power on any terms which
 i) are prudent and publicly defensible for us, at home, in the Commonwealth, and generally;
 ii) the United States will agree to?
At first this seems hopeless. But since I think it is the one thing which will persuade de Gaulle to accept a European settlement – not merely in the economic field of Sixes and Sevens (which is vital), but in the general association of the British, with other Governments, in a Confederal system – I think it is worth serious examination ...

33. ... Could Britain and France form a nuclear force – sharing the cost, production, etc. – as European trustees for NATO?
 Could we devise a formula for joint political control by us both? Failing that, could we at least have some arrangement for consultation about its

use, on the analogy of President Eisenhower's *private* understanding with me? Either of these arrangements could extend, not only to the NATO area, but throughout the world.

Could we thus give France the satisfaction of a nominally 'independent nuclear force' while subjecting them to at least the same kind of moral restraints which the Americans have accepted in their understanding with us?

34. I think we should give urgent study to this and see if we can devise a workable plan – which (at the right moment) we could get the United States to accept and which we could then use to win de Gaulle over.

With Kennedy, I would be quite straight. I would tell him I wanted his agreement

  a) because, if we ever settle a *Test* Agreement, we shall have to do something about France;
  b) because only if he can help me to do a deal with de Gaulle, can we keep Britain in Europe and relieve the United States of some of their burden ...

With de Gaulle also it would be a deal – but quite an honourable one. It would be the reconstituting of a fully united Europe – united economically, politically and militarily, and at the same time securing for France (through Tripartitism) an equal place with Britain in discussing *world* affairs with our American friends ...

Memorandum by the Prime Minister, 29 December 1960–3 January 1961. PRO Prem 11/3325.

DOCUMENT 22   APPLYING FOR MEMBERSHIP OF THE EEC

In July 1960 the Cabinet rehearsed the arguments for and against Britain joining the EEC.

The Chancellor of the Exchequer (Derick Heathcoat Amory) [said that] a decision to join the Community would be essentially a political act with economic consequences, rather than an economic act with political consequences. The arguments for joining the Community were strong. If we remained outside it, our political influence in Europe and in the rest of the world was likely to decline. By joining it we should not only avoid tariff discrimination by its members against our exports, but should also be able to participate in a large and rapidly expanding market. However, the arguments against United Kingdom membership were also very strong. We should be surrendering independent control of our commercial policies to a

European *bloc*, when our trading interests were world-wide. We should have to abandon our special economic relationship with the Commonwealth, including free entry for Commonwealth goods and the preferential system, and should instead be obliged to discriminate actively against the Commonwealth. We should have to devise for agriculture and horticulture new policies under which the burden of support for the farmers would be largely transferred from the Exchequer to the consumer, thus increasing the cost of living. Finally, we should sacrifice our loyalties and obligations to the members of the European Free Trade Association (E.F.T.A.), some of which would find it impossible to join the E.E.C. as full members.

There were four possible courses for the United Kingdom. The first would be to seek full membership of the Community on the terms of the Treaty of Rome. This was wholly unacceptable, if only because it involved discriminating against the fundamental trading interests of the Commonwealth and in favour of Europe. Secondly, we could seek to negotiate membership of the Community on special terms. Though we should have to accept in general the common tariff on the Community, we could seek to preserve some free entry for Commonwealth foodstuffs. But, if we were to pursue this course, we should have to accept the fact that our preferential position in the Commonwealth (which affected 20 per cent of our total exports and was considered by industry to be still of substantial value) would be progressively eroded. Thirdly, we might seek some form of association with the Community falling short of full membership. This course might be easier for the other members of E.F.T.A. but it would not enable us to exert as much influence in the Community as if we were members of it. Finally, we could stay outside the E.E.C. and consolidate the E.F.T.A. In the end, we might have to accept this last course, but we had never visualised it as more than a second best to a wider European system.

The Chancellor said that his personal conclusion was that we should be ready to join the Community if we could do so without substantially impairing our relations with the Commonwealth. We might seek to persuade the other Commonwealth countries to relinquish some of their special advantages in the United Kingdom market in order to enable us either to accept membership of the Community on special terms or to enter into some form of association with it. But we should not press that persuasion to the point where it threatened the Commonwealth relationship. ... We should try to carry our partners in the E.F.T.A. with us.

Cabinet Minutes, 13 July 1960. PRO CAB 128/34.

DOCUMENT 23   1952 DEFENCE POLICY REVIEW

The Chiefs of Staff responded to Churchill's request for a review of defence costs with a report recommending that Britain's strategy should be based on nuclear weapons.

10. We believe that, during the first weeks following any Soviet aggression, Russia would be subjected to such a devastating attack upon so high a proportion of her vital centres that she would be unlikely to survive it as a Power capable of waging a full scale war ...

12. ... It is now clear that there is in the foreseeable future no effective defence against atomic air attack ...

21. We conclude that war is unlikely provided that the Cold War is conducted by the Allies in a patient, levelheaded and determined manner ...

36. The first essential of allied policy must be to establish and maintain as long as may be necessary a really effective deterrent against war ...

38. ... The Allies must give the necessary priority to the air striking forces, both where and when necessary ...

39. ... It must be made clear to the Russians that the Allies are able to make their advance across Europe both slow and difficult – a state of affairs which we are now approaching. This element of the deterrent must be provided by a sufficiency of land and air forces at a high state of readiness in Western Europe, supported by atomic air power ...

41. ... The fact is that the Free World cannot hope, spread out as it is in an attenuated ring round the great mass of Russia and China, to contain the enemy by land forces deprived of support by atomic weapons. The Free World can maintain superior strength, and thus prevent the outbreak of war, only by matching science against man-power. We suggest that the existence of the great atomic deterrent is of vital importance to humanity and freedom to use it must be maintained ...

Defence Policy and Global Strategy, 17 June 1952. PRO CAB 131/12.

DOCUMENT 24   THE SANDYS WHITE PAPER

*The Macmillan government carried out a major review of defence policy.
Duncan Sandys's White Paper continued to emphasise the central role of
nuclear weapons and recommended large cuts in Britain's conventional
forces and the ending of conscription.*

12. It must be frankly recognised that there is at present no means of
providing adequate protection for the people of this country against the
consequences of an attack with nuclear weapons ...

13. This makes it more than ever clear that the overriding consideration in
all military planning must be to prevent war rather than to prepare for it ...

15. The free world is to-day mainly dependent for its protection upon the
nuclear capacity of the United States. While Britain cannot by comparison
make more than a modest contribution, there is a wide measure of
agreement that she must possess an appreciable element of nuclear deterrent
power of her own. British atomic bombs are already in steady production
and the Royal Air Force holds a substantial number of them. A British
megaton weapon has now been developed. This will shortly be tested and
thereafter a stock will be manufactured.

16. The means of delivering these weapons is provided at present by
medium bombers of the V-class. ... It is the intention that these should be
supplemented by ballistic rockets. Agreement in principle has recently been
reached with the United States Government for the supply of some
medium-range missiles of this type ...

22. ... The strength of the British Army of the Rhine will be reduced from
about 77,000 to about 64,000 during the next twelve months; and, subject
to consultation with the Allied Governments in the autumn, further
reductions will be made thereafter. The force will be reorganised in such a
way as to increase the proportion of fighting units; the atomic rocket
artillery will be introduced which will greatly augment their fire-power.

23. The aircraft of the Second Tactical Air Force in Germany will be
reduced to about half their present number by the end of March, 1958 ...

34. With the reduction in the size of garrisons and other British forces overseas,
it is more than ever essential to be able to despatch reinforcements at short
notice. With this object, a Central Reserve will be maintained in the British Isles.

35. To be effective, the Central Reserve must possess the means of rapid
mobility. For this purpose, a substantial fleet of transport aircraft is being
built up in R.A.F. Transport Command ...

38. ... It is proposed to base the main elements of the Royal Navy upon a small number of carrier groups, each composed of one aircraft carrier and a number of supporting ships. ... The policy will be to rely on a reduced number of more modern ships, some of which will be equipped with guided missiles ...

42. The revised defence plan, with its greatly reduced demands on manpower and its emphasis on highly trained mobile forces, now makes it possible to contemplate putting the Services on to an all-regular basis; and the Government will endeavour to bring about this change as soon as practicable ...

45. ... The combined strength of the three Services is now about 690,000. During the next twelve months, it is proposed to reduce it to about 625,000 ...

46. ... The Government ... have concluded that it would be right to aim at stabilising the armed forces on an all-regular footing at a strength of about 375,000 by the end of 1962 ...

47. The Government have accordingly decided to plan on the basis that there will be no further call-up under the National Service Acts after the end of 1960.

72. ... It can safely be assumed that the new plan, when it is fully implemented, will further appreciably reduce the burden on the economy.

'Defence: Outline of Future Policy', Cmnd.124, February 1957, PP (1956–57) XXIII.

DOCUMENT 25 **MACMILLAN ON ECONOMIC AND COLONIAL POLICY**

In the early 1950s, government ministers were reluctant to address Britain's economic problems by reducing overseas commitments. Macmillan, Housing Minister from 1951 to 1954, proposed to the Cabinet that Britain should develop the Sterling Area as a trading bloc to serve Britain's needs.

II. 1. Our economic survival in the next year or two will largely depend upon world confidence in sterling. This will depend, among other things, upon our ability to maintain ourselves as a Great Power ...

II. 2. ... Any serious reduction in real power is more likely to hinder than to assist our eventual recovery. Britain can only maintain a population of 50 million in safety as a Great Power; and to be a Great Power in the world as it is to-day, her armaments must be in good order ... .

IV. Our aims, therefore, should be:-

To reduce still further ... our imports from the dollar area and other areas with which we are in deficit, and, where necessary, to substitute for them imports from the sterling area. ... We should try, even at the cost of severe sacrifices in the short-term, to produce inside the sterling area the goods we need ...

V. 3. ... We shall also have to resort to more drastic forms of control by discriminatory quota and licence. ... Priority should be given to sterling produce as a declared permanent policy. This, of course, involves exercising our right to free ourselves from the limitations imposed by G.A.T.T. ...

X. We are faced at home with a steady intensification of class divisions and that sense of frustration which leads to the rejection of all established institutions; we may have to face at the same time the break-up of the Commonwealth and our decline into a second-rate Power. I see no escape from these dangers except by the fearless proclamation of a policy which will reinspire the masses and restore their pride and confidence.

This is the choice – the slide into a shoddy and slushy Socialism, or the march to the third British Empire.

'Economic Policy', Cabinet Memorandum by the Housing Minister, 17 June 1952. PRO CAB 129/52.

DOCUMENT 26 **POLICY ON MALAYA**

Like the Labour government before them, the Conservatives were determined to defeat the communist insurgents in Malaya.

There was a growing, but still insufficient, general recognition of the importance of South-East Asia to the Commonwealth. One way of measuring this importance was to consider the economic and strategic implications of Communist control, and in particular the implications for our own territories. The danger of Communism lay, not in its appeal to the peoples of the area, nor primarily, perhaps, in the possibilities of armed aggression, but in the number of issues – racial, religious and political – which were ripe for exploitation by troublemakers and seekers after power. But the dangers of further armed aggression should not be under-estimated and precautionary plans must be made.

The area possessed considerable economic resources which could provide a substantial access of strength to world Communism. The rice of Siam and

Burma was of the greatest importance to our own territories, and for this and other reasons, Communist success would, moreover, have important political and psychological effects throughout the whole Far East.

The Communist threat must be met with military, economic, and political weapons: our aim must be to promote stability, confidence and prosperity, throughout the area ...

The countries of South-East Asia recognised that they were dependent on foreign aid, but they were nevertheless, suspicious of the implications of receiving it. In particular they feared United States economic domination.

There had been a great revival of interest in the United Nations since the United Nations action in Korea which had ... proved, against all expectation, that collective measures of defence might succeed ...

The immediate objectives for South-East Asia must be:- ... to secure a closer co-ordination of policy with the United States on China and Japan, and indeed on Far Eastern matters generally; to ensure that there was no relaxation of our effort in South-East Asia, despite the general cry for retrenchment; ... and to secure a clear policy towards Malaya so that no doubts would remain among the public there about our ultimate intentions ...

Our policy of guiding Malaya towards self-government within the Commonwealth had been repeatedly stated and had been reasserted by the Colonial Secretary ...

The difficulties of presenting our policy were increased by the divergent interests of the Malay and Chinese communities in Malaya. ... The main doubt among the people related, not to our intentions in Malaya, but to our physical capacity for carrying them out.

Minutes of Cabinet Far East Committee, 8 January 1952. PRO CAB 134/897.

DOCUMENT 27 THE CREATION OF THE CENTRAL AFRICAN FEDERATION

The Central African Federation was created in 1953. It comprised Northern Rhodesia, Southern Rhodesia and Nyasaland.

7. From the economic point of view there are the strongest arguments in favour of closer association. The economies of the Central African territories are linked by a common port at Beira for all three of them; a common railway system for the two Rhodesias; the dependence of copper mining in Northern Rhodesia on coal from Southern Rhodesia; the dependence of the two Rhodesias on manpower from Nyasaland; and the Zambesi and Shire river basin with its great potentialities for the development of hydro-electric power on a Central African basis. ... This development ought to proceed on a Central African basis so that the

resources of the whole region may best be devoted to economic advancement ...

8. From the political point of view the need for closer association is even more urgent. ... We are faced in Central Africa with pressure by a country far stronger economically and industrially than any of the Central African territories, led by a militant Nationalist party with expansionist aims, anxious to strengthen its influence in the north. ... Positive steps must be taken to resist it and by far the most effective step would be active support for federation by His Majesty's Government.

10. ... Amalgamation ... would be bitterly and violently opposed by African opinion in Northern Rhodesia and Nyasaland and in our view would be quite unjustifiable.

11. ... We are convinced that federation is the right solution. ... Certainly federation is the only form of closer association to which there is any chance of securing African agreement or acquiescence ...

Cabinet Memorandum by Commonwealth Secretary and Colonial Secretary, 9 November 1951. PRO CAB 129/48.

DOCUMENT 28   MACMILLAN'S WIND OF CHANGE SPEECH

Macmillan's tour of Africa in 1960 was a symbol of his government's recognition of the need to hasten the pace of decolonisation.

The most striking of all the impressions I have formed since I left London a month ago is of the strength of ... African national consciousness. In different places it takes different forms but it is happening everywhere. The wind of change is blowing through this continent and, whether we like it or not, this growth of national consciousness is a political fact. We must all accept it as a fact, and our national policies must take account of it ... .
     I sincerely believe that if we cannot do so we may imperil the precarious balance between the East and West on which the peace of the world depends ... .
     As a fellow member of the Commonwealth it is our earnest desire to give South Africa our support and encouragement, but I hope you will not mind my saying frankly that there are some aspects of your policies which make it impossible for us to do this without being false to our own deep convictions about the political destinies of free men to which in our own territories we are trying to give effect.

Macmillan's speech to the South African Parliament, 3 February 1960, [7], pp. 522–31.

DOCUMENT 29   WELENSKY'S REACTION TO THE
MONCKTON COMMISSION REPORT

Macmillan established the Monckton Commission to advise on the future of the Central African Federation. Its report, published in October 1960, incensed Sir Roy Welensky, the Prime Minister of the CAF.

While Mr. Sandys [Commonwealth Secretary] was on his travels, I wrote to Iain Macleod [Colonial Secretary] on September 16th ...

'I have now had a chance to study the Monckton Report. I will, of course, be discussing it next week with Sandys. As I anticipated from the beginning, the report is a disaster. Its mere publication will make the continuation of federation virtually impossible. Almost without exception, its recommendations play into the hands of African extremists and its philosophy of appeasement will rule out any possibility of reasonable changes being made on merit. The secession proposals are the final straw and I consider them to be a complete breach of the understandings upon which I agreed to the appointment of the Commission ...

'We are in the midst of events which I believe will, if not very carefully handled, lead to the end of civilised and responsible government in this part of Africa before very long.'...

The Monckton Report was published at six o'clock in the evening, our time, on Tuesday October 11th. ... Though for two years longer they continued to deny it most vehemently, those who had created the Federation of Rhodesia and Nyasaland at this moment passed sentence of death on it ...

The British Government wanted it all done smoothly, with a lot of noble sentiments, no harsh wind of truth, the maximum appeasement of the African nationalists and their backers in the United Nations, in America and in Britain, and the minimum financial cost and moral and political discredit for themselves. I was not prepared to play it their way and give in tamely. Henceforth I suspected every move they made, and I did my best to fight every inch of ground they tried to gain.

Welensky, [131], pp. 271–2, 282–4.

APPENDIX 1: GENERAL ELECTION RESULTS

Party	Seats	Candidates	Votes	% of vote
1951 (25 Oct)				
Conservative	321	617	13,717,538	48.6
Liberal	6	109	730,556	2.5
Labour	295	617	13,948,605	48.8
Others	3	33	198,969	0.7
Turnout: 82.5%				
1955 (26 May)				
Conservative	344	623	13,286,569	49.7
Liberal	6	110	722,405	2.7
Labour	277	620	12,404,970	46.4
Others	3	56	346,554	1.2
Turnout: 76.7%				
1959 (8 Oct)				
Conservative	365	625	13,749,830	49.4
Liberal	6	216	1,638,571	5.9
Labour	258	621	12,215,538	43.8
Others	1	74	142,670	0.9
Turnout: 78.8%				
1964 (15 Oct)				
Conservative	304	630	12,001,396	43.4
Liberal	9	365	3,092,878	11.2
Labour	317	628	12,205,814	44.1
Others	0	134	347,905	1.3
Turnout: 77.1%				

APPENDIX 2: PRINCIPAL GOVERNMENT MINISTERS, 1951–64

Prime Minister	Date of appointment
Winston Churchill	26 October 1951
Anthony Eden	6 April 1955
Harold Macmillan	10 January 1957
Alec Douglas-Home	18 October 1963

Foreign Secretary	
Anthony Eden	28 October 1951
Harold Macmillan	7 April 1955
Selwyn Lloyd	20 December 1955
Earl of Home	27 July 1960
R.A. Butler	20 October 1963

Chancellor of the Exchequer	
RA Butler	28 October 1951
Harold Macmillan	20 December 1955
Peter Thorneycroft	13 January 1957
Derick Heathcoat-Amory	6 January 1958
Selwyn Lloyd	27 July 1960
Reginald Maudling	13 July 1962

Home Secretary	
David Maxwell-Fyfe	28 October 1951
Gwilym Lloyd George	18 October 1954
R.A. Butler	13 January 1957
Henry Brooke	13 July 1962

Minister of Defence	
Winston Churchill	28 October 1951
Earl Alexander of Tunis	1 March 1952

Minister of Defence (cont)	Date of appointment
Harold Macmillan	18 October 1954
Selwyn Lloyd	7 April 1955
Walter Monckton	20 December 1955
Antony Head	18 October 1956
Duncan Sandys	13 January 1957
Harold Watkinson	14 October 1959
Peter Thorneycroft	13 July 1962

Colonial Secretary

Oliver Lyttelton	28 October 1951
Alan Lennox-Boyd	28 July 1954
Iain Macleod	14 October 1959
Reginald Maudling	9 October 1961
Duncan Sandys	13 July 1962

Commonwealth Secretary

Lord Ismay	28 October 1951
Marquis of Salisbury	12 March 1952
Viscount Swinton	24 November 1952
Earl of Home	7 April 1955
Duncan Sandys	27 July 1960

BIBLIOGRAPHY

DOCUMENT COLLECTIONS AND REFERENCE WORKS

1 D Butler and G Butler *British Political Facts, 1900–1994*, Macmillan (7th edition) 1994

2 L Butler and H Jones (eds) *Britain in the Twentieth Century, A Documentary Reader, Volume 2 1939–1970*, Heinemann 1995

3 AH Halsey (ed.) *British Social Trends since 1900*, Macmillan (2nd edition) 1988

4 Hansard *Parliamentary Debates, House of Commons*, Official Report, 5th Series, volumes 493–700

5 PJ Madgwick, D Steeds, LJ Williams *Britain since 1945*, Hutchinson 1982

6 R Ovendale *British Defence Policy since 1945*, Manchester University Press 1994

7 AN Porter and AJ Stockwell (eds) *British Imperial Policy and Decolonization, Volume 2 1951–64*, Macmillan 1989

GENERAL HISTORIES

8 R Blake *The Decline of Power 1914–1964*, Paladin 1986

9 V Bogdanor and R Skidelsky (eds) *The Age of Affluence 1951–1964*, Macmillan 1970

10 D Childs *Britain since 1945*, Routledge (3rd edition) 1992

11 D Childs *Britain since 1939, Progress and Decline*, Macmillan 1995

12 T Gourvish and A O'Day (eds) *Britain since 1945*, Macmillan 1991

13 T Gorst, L Johnman, WS Lucas (eds) *Post-War Britain, Themes and Perspectives 1945–64*, Pinter 1989

14 T Gorst, L Johnman, WS Lucas (eds) *Contemporary British History 1931–61, Politics and the Limits of Policy*, Pinter 1991

15 TO Lloyd *Empire, Welfare State, Europe: English History 1906–1992*, Oxford University Press (4th edition) 1993

16 A Marwick *Britain since 1945*, Penguin 1990

17 KO Morgan *The People's Peace, British History 1945–1989*, Oxford 1990

18 K Robbins *The Eclipse of a Great Power, Modern Britain 1870–1992*, Longman (2nd edition) 1994

19   A Sked and C Cook *Post-War Britain, A Political History
     1945–1992*, Penguin (4th edition) 1993
20   LM Smith (ed.) *The Making of Britain: Echoes of Greatness*,
     Macmillan 1988

BIOGRAPHIES, AUTOBIOGRAPHIES AND DIARIES

21   Lord Butler *The Art of the Possible*, Hamish Hamilton 1971
22   J Callaghan *Time and Chance*, Collins 1987
23   J Campbell *Nye Bevan and the Mirage of British Socialism*,
     Weidenfeld and Nicolson 1987
24   J Campbell *Edward Heath*, Jonathan Cape 1993
25   D Carlton *Anthony Eden*, Allen Lane 1981, Unwin Paperbacks, 1986
26   J Charmley (ed.) *Descent to Suez, Diaries of Evelyn Shuckburgh,
     1951–1956*, Weidenfeld and Nicolson 1986
27   Sir A Eden *Full Circle*, Cassell 1960
28   M Foot *Aneurin Bevan, Volume 2 1945–1960*, Davis-Poynter 1973
29   M Gilbert *Churchill, A Life*, Heinemann 1991
30   M Gilbert *Never Despair, Winston Churchill: Official Biography,
     Volume 8*, Heinemann 1988
31   D Healey *The Time of My Life*, Michael Joseph, 1989
32   A Horne *Macmillan: Official Biography, Volume 1, 1894–1956*,
     Macmillan 1988
33   A Horne *Macmillan: Official Biography, Volume 2, 1957–1986*,
     Macmillan 1989
34   A Howard *RAB, The Life of RA Butler*, Jonathan Cape 1987
35   R Rhodes James *Anthony Eden*, Weidenfeld and Nicolson 1986
36   H Macmillan *Tides of Fortune 1945–55, Memoirs Volume 3*,
     Macmillan 1969
37   H Macmillan *Riding the Storm 1956–1959, Memoirs Volume 4*,
     Macmillan 1971
38   H Macmillan *Pointing the Way 1959–1961, Memoirs Volume 5*,
     Macmillan 1972
39   H Macmillan *At the End of the Day 1961–1963, Memoirs Volume
     6*, Macmillan 1973
40   Lord Moran *Winston Churchill: The Struggle for Survival
     1940–1965*, Sphere 1968
41   J Morgan (ed.) *The Backbench Diaries of Richard Crossman*,
     Hamish Hamilton/Jonathan Cape 1981
42   H Pelling *Winston Churchill*, Macmillan 1974
43   B Pimlott *Harold Wilson*, HarperCollins 1992
44   C Ponting *Churchill*, Sinclair-Stevenson 1994
45   V Rothwell *Anthony Eden, A Political Biography*, Manchester
     University Press 1992
46   A Sampson *Macmillan, A Study in Ambiguity*, Pelican 1968

47   DR Thorpe *Selwyn Lloyd,* Jonathan Cape 1989
48   J Turner *Macmillan,* Longman 1994
49   PM Williams *Hugh Gaitskell,* Oxford University Press 1982
50   PM Williams (ed.) *The Diary of Hugh Gaitskell 1945–1956,*
      Jonathan Cape 1983

DOMESTIC POLITICS

51   K Alderman 'Harold Macmillan's "Night of the Long Knives" ',
      Contemporary Record, Vol. 6, No. 2, 1992
52   BWE Alford *British Economic Performance 1945–1975,* Macmillan 1988
53   S Brittan *The Treasury under the Tories,* Secker and Warburg 1964
54   D Butler *British General Elections since 1945,* Basil Blackwell 1989
55   A Cairncross 'The Postwar Years 1945–77' in R Floud and D
      McCloskey (eds) *The Economic History of Britain since 1700,*
      Volume 2 1860 to the 1970s, Cambridge University Press 1981
56   P Clarke *A Question of Leadership,* Hamish Hamilton 1991,
      Penguin 1992
57   C Cook *A Short History of the Liberal Party 1900–1988,* Macmillan
      (3rd edition) 1989
58   J Davis Smith *The Attlee and Churchill Administrations and
      Industrial Unrest, 1945–1955,* Pinter 1990
59   M Dintenfass *The Decline of Industrial Britain,* Routledge 1992
60   JCR Dow *The Management of the British Economy 1945–1960,*
      Cambridge University Press 1965
61   D Dutton *British Politics since 1945, The Rise and Fall of
      Consensus,* Basil Blackwell 1991
62   PA Hall 'The State and Economic Decline', in B Elbaum, W Lazonick
      (eds) *The Decline of the British Economy,* Oxford University Press
      1986
63   P Hennessy and A Seldon (eds) *Ruling Performance, British
      Governments from Attlee to Thatcher,* Basil Blackwell 1987
64   M Jenkins *Bevanism, Labour's High Noon,* Spokesman 1979
65   D Kavanagh and P Morris *Consensus Politics from Attlee to
      Thatcher,* Basil Blackwell 1989
66   R Lamb *The Macmillan Years 1957–1963, The Emerging Truth,*
      John Murray 1995
67   K Laybourn *A History of British Trade Unionism,* Alan Sutton 1992
68   K Middlemass *Power, Competition and the State, Volume 1 Britain
      in Search of Balance 1940–1961,* Macmillan 1986
69   KO Morgan *Labour People,* Oxford University Press 1987
70   GC Peden *British Economic and Social Policy, Lloyd George to
      Margaret Thatcher,* Philip Allan 1985
71   H Pelling *A Short History of the Labour Party,* Macmillan (9th
      edition) 1991

72 H Pelling *A History of British Trade Unionism*, Penguin (5th edition) 1992

73 S Pollard *The Development of the British Economy 1914–90*, Edward Arnold (4th edition) 1992

74 SJ Proctor 'Floating Convertibility, The Emergence of the Robot Plan 1951–52', *Contemporary Record*, Vol. 7, No. 1, 1993

75 J Ramsden 'Conservatives since 1945', *Contemporary Record*, Vol. 2, No. 1, 1988

76 J Ramsden *A History of the Conservative Party: The Age of Churchill and Eden 1940–57*, Longman 1995

77 A Roberts *Eminent Churchillians*, Weidenfeld and Nicolson 1994

78 N Rollings 'British Budgetary Policy 1945–1954', *Economic History Review*, Vol. XLI, 1988

79 A Seldon *Churchill's Indian Summer, The Conservative Government 1951–1955*, Hodder and Stoughton 1981

80 A Seldon and S Ball (eds) *Conservative Century, The Conservative Party since 1900*, Oxford University Press 1994

81 A Sked *Britain's Decline, Problems and Perspectives*, Basil Blackwell 1987

82 J Tomlinson 'A Keynesian Revolution in Economic Policy-Making', *Economic History Review*, 2nd series, Vol. XXXVII, 1984

83 P Warwick 'Did Britain Change?', *Journal of Contemporary History*, Vol. 20, No. 1, 1985

84 MJ Wiener *English Culture and the Decline of the Industrial Spirit 1850–1980*, Cambridge University Press 1981

85 GDN Worswick and PH Ady (eds) *The British Economy in the 1950s*, Oxford University Press 1962

FOREIGN, DEFENCE AND IMPERIAL POLICY

86 PJ Cain and AG Hopkins *British Imperialism, Crisis and Deconstruction 1914–1990*, Longman 1993

87 D Carlton *Britain and the Suez Crisis*, Basil Blackwell 1988

88 ME Chamberlain *Decolonization, The Fall of European Empires*, Basil Blackwell 1985

89 C Cross *The Fall of the British Empire*, Hodder and Stoughton 1968

90 J Darwin *Britain and Decolonisation*, Macmillan 1988

91 J Darwin *The End of the British Empire*, Basil Blackwell 1991

92 J Darwin 'British Decolonisation since 1945', *Journal of Imperial and Commonwealth History*, Vol. XIII, No. 2, January 1984, pp. 187–209

93 M Dockrill *British Defence since 1945*, Basil Blackwell 1988

94 M Dockrill and JW Young (eds) *British Foreign Policy, 1945–56*, Macmillan 1989

95 D Dutton 'Anticipating Maastricht: The Conservative Party and Britain's First Application to join the European Community', *Contemporary Record*, Vol. 7, No. 3, 1993

96 M Fawzi *Suez 1956, An Egyptian Perspective*, Shorouk 1986

97 R Fullick and G Powell *Suez, The Double War*, Hamish Hamilton 1979

98 F Furedi 'Britain's Colonial Emergencies', *Journal of Historical Sociology*, Vol. 2, No. 3, 1989

99 S George *Britain and European Integration since 1945*, Basil Blackwell 1991

100 P Gifford and WR Louis (eds) *The Transfer of Power in Africa, Decolonisation 1940–60*, Yale University Press 1988

101 D Goldsworthy *Colonial Issues in British Politics 1945–61*, Oxford University Press 1971

102 D Goldsworthy 'Keeping Change within Bounds, Colonial Policy during the Churchill and Eden Governments 1951–57', *Journal of Imperial and Commonwealth History*, Vol. XVIII, No. 1, January 1990, pp. 81–108

103 S Greenwood *Britain and European Cooperation since 1945*, Basil Blackwell 1992

104 MH Heikal *Cutting the Lion's Tail, Suez through Egyptian Eyes*, Andre Deutsch 1986

105 RF Holland *European Decolonization 1918–1981*, Macmillan 1985

106 RF Holland 'The Imperial Factor in British Strategies from Attlee to Macmillan', *Journal of Imperial and Commonwealth History*, Vol. XIII, No. 2, January 1984

107 P Kennedy *The Realities Behind Diplomacy*, Fontana 1981

108 G Krozewski 'Sterling, the "Minor" Territories and the End of Formal Empire 1939–58', *Economic History Review*, Vol. XLVI, 1993

109 K Kyle *Suez*, Weidenfeld and Nicolson 1991

110 R Lamb *The Failure of the Eden Government*, Sidgwick and Jackson 1987

111 B Lapping *End of Empire*, Granada 1985

112 S Lloyd *Suez 1956, A Personal Account*, Jonathan Cape 1978

113 TO Lloyd *The British Empire 1558–1983*, Oxford University Press 1984

114 WR Louis 'American Anti-Colonialism and the Dissolution of the British Empire', *International Affairs*, Vol. 61, No. 3, 1985

115 WR Louis and R Owen (eds) *Suez 1956, The Crisis and its Consequences*, Oxford University Press 1989

116 WR Louis and R Robinson 'The Imperialism of Decolonization', *Journal of Imperial and Commonwealth History*, Vol. XXII, No. 3, September 1994, pp. 462–511

117 A Low, B Lapping, RF Holland 'Did Suez Hasten the End of Empire?', *Contemporary Record*, Vol. 1, No. 2, 1987 and Vol. 1, No. 4, 1988

118 WS Lucas *Divided We Stand, Britain, the US and the Suez Crisis*, Hodder and Stoughton 1991

119 J Melissen 'The Restoration of the Nuclear Alliance, Great Britain and Atomic Negotiations with the United States 1957–58', *Contemporary Record*, Vol. 6, No. 1, 1992

120 FS Northedge *Descent from Power, British Foreign Policy 1945–1973*, Allen and Unwin 1974

121 A Nutting *No End of a Lesson, The Story of Suez*, Constable 1967

122 AN Porter (ed.) *Atlas of British Overseas Expansion*, Routledge 1991

123 B Porter *The Lion's Share*, Longman (2nd edition) 1984

124 D Reynolds *Britannia Overruled, British Policy and World Power in the 20th Century*, Longman 1991

125 C Schenk 'The Sterling Area and British Policy Alternatives in the 1950s', *Contemporary Record*, Vol. 6, No. 2, 1992

126 AM Schlesinger Jnr *A Thousand Days*, Andre Deutsch, 1965

127 E Spiers 'The British Nuclear Deterrent' in D Dilks (ed.) *Retreat from Power, Volume 2*, Macmillan 1981

128 AJ Stockwell 'British Imperial Policy and Decolonisation in Malaya', *Journal of Imperial and Commonwealth History*, Vol. XIII, No. 1, October 1984

129 H Thomas *The Suez Affair*, Weidenfeld and Nicolson (2nd edition) 1986

130 BR Tomlinson 'National Decline and the Loss of Empire', *Journal of Imperial and Commonwealth History*, Vol. 9, No. 1, 1982

131 Sir R Welensky *4000 Days*, Collins 1964

132 JW Young (ed.) *The Foreign Policy of Churchill's Peacetime Administration, 1951–55*, Leicester University Press 1988

INDEX

Aden, 66, 71, 91
Africa, 38, 57, 73, 74, 75, 76, 78–89, 98, 100
Algeria, 50
Amery, Julian, Conservative politician, 56
Amory, Derick Heathcoat, Chancellor of the Exchequer, 31–3
Arab-Israeli War 1948–49, 47
Arden-Clarke, Sir Charles, Gold Coast governor, 79
Attlee, Clement, Labour PM, 1, 2, 11, 14, 15, 16, 66, 96, 97
Australia, 43, 92
Austria, 46

Baghdad Pact, 48, 58, 59, 90
Banda, Dr Hastings, 85, 87
Bank of England, 25, 30
Bay of Pigs, 61
Beeching Report, 10–11, 96
Belgian Congo, 76, 86
Benelux, 46
Bevan, Aneurin, Labour politician, 14–18, 21
Birch, Nigel, Treasury minister, 31
Blue Streak missile, 18, 19, 63, 69, 100
Braddock, Bessie, Labour politician, 13
Briggs, General Sir Harold, 77
British Guiana, 92
Brown, George, deputy Labour leader, 21
Budgets:
   1951, 14
   1952, 26

1953, 27
1954, 27–8
1955, 2, 28
1955 supplementary, 29
1956, 30
1957, 31
1958, 31–2
1959, 32
1960, 32
1961, 33
1961 supplementary, 33–4
1962, 34–5
1963, 36
Bulganin, Nikolai Aleksandrovich, Russian leader, 46, 54
Burma, 72
Butler, R.A., 3, 11, 88
   as Chancellor of the Exchequer, 2, 23, 25–30, 46
   as Foreign Secretary, 64
   as Home Secretary, 11
Butskellism, consensus economics, 23–25, 28, 30

Callaghan, James, Labour politician, 37
Campaign for Nuclear Disarmament (CND), 19, 58, 70
Canada, 53
Capital punishment, 11
Castro, Fidel, Cuban leader, 61
Central African Federation, 83, 86, 87, 88
Central Treaty Organisation (CENTO), 59
Ceylon, 72
Challe, General Maurice, 51, 52

RELATED TITLES

Paul Adelman, *Gladstone, Disraeli and Later Victorian Politics* Second Edition (1983)   0 582 35332 7

Dr Adelman takes as his theme, in this authoritative study of late-Victorian politics, the development of the two-party system. He shows how the Liberals and Conservatives organised themselves, and considers who supported them and why. He also discusses the influence of leadership and policy on their fortunes, and analyses their performance in general elections.

Paul Adelman, *The Decline of the Liberal Party, 1910–1931* Second Edition (1995)   0 582 27733 7

In 1906 the Liberals formed one of the most brilliant administrations in the history of twentieth-century Britain. Thereafter, however, the party went into a decline from which it has never really recovered. In this concise, popular study (now revised and reset) Paul Adelman seeks to explain this curious political phenomenon.

Stuart Ball, *The Conservative Party and British Politics 1902–1951* (1995)   0 582 08002 9

'Stuart Ball has produced a book of value to anyone interested in exploring the historical roots of current arguments, and one which is highly recommended.'   *Polity Scene*

The history of the Conservative Party during the first half of the twentieth century was marked by crisis and controversy, from Joseph Chamberlain's tariff reform campaign through the Lloyd George coalition and the National Government between the wars to the defeat of 1945 and the post-war recovery. This new study provides a lucid account of this turbulent and formative period in the history of the most durable and adaptive force in modern British politics.

Kevin Jeffreys, *The Attlee Governments, 1945–1951* (1992)
0 582 06105 9

In 1945 the Labour government under Clement Attlee set about a major transformation of British society. In his succinct but comprehensive study, Dr Jeffreys analyses the main changes and relates them to debates within the Labour party on the nature of its aims and how best to achieve them. He relates his analysis to a wide range of documentary material drawn from the ever increasing volume of primary sources for the period.